"An honest book about the courageous journey toward self-love. I would recommend *Store Bought Baby* for anyone who's struggling to find their voice or feels misunderstood in any way."

—Kimberly Kingsley, LPC
Author of *Portals of Peace: A Path to Inner Peace and a Healed World*, and *The Energy Cure*

"I am mesmerized by *Store Bought Baby*—a raw and beautiful memoir. Laura Melane's story made me feel profoundly seen in ways I didn't expect. She writes with such honesty, vulnerability, and grace that I couldn't put it down. Her memoir is a rare gift that gives voice to the unspoken experiences so many of us carry. If you're looking for a book that will move, comfort, and inspire you to find your voice—one that will change you and remind you of the power you have to choose yourself every day—*Store Bought Baby* is a must-read."

—Jane Cebrynski
Founder, Empower for Growth: Transforming high achievers into champions of their lives

"You don't need to be adopted for this story to stir something in your soul. Laura Melane recounts her experiences with such refreshing authenticity that the story grips and holds you from beginning to end. She takes you on her journey in search of answers to questions we all struggle with—who are we deep inside? How did the child we *were* become the adult we *are*? *Store Bought Baby* will strike a chord, awaken long-forgotten feelings, and just may help you complete your own personal puzzle."

—Mona Botros
Journalist and Documentary Filmmaker

"I love books that make me think, move me emotionally, or teach me new perspectives. *Store Bought Baby* accomplishes all three. Laura's courage to share her journey from adoption through adulthood and its affects upon her health, career, relationships, marriage, parenting, and life was educational, emotional, and inspiring. I highly recommend it, especially for men like me to better understand women's experience and perspective."

—Jerry Banks
Real Estate Investor, Entrepreneur,
and author of *Eat Sh*t and Smile*

"Laura Melane's memoir is a powerful story of resilience, strength, and courage. In *Store Bought Baby*, she bravely and skillfully shares her own life lessons about overcoming the 'good girl trap.' She shows how she successfully navigated the internal conflicts she must overcome, learning to stand up for herself, set healthy boundaries, and ultimately reject relationships that brought chaos and turmoil into her life, all while showing grace and compassion for those around her."

—Aida Sibic
Author of *Luck Follows the Brave*

"*Store Bought Baby* provides an in-depth account of one woman's experience being adopted as a baby, finding her birth mother, and, through self-reflection, ultimately coming to peace with herself. Kudos to Laura Melane for vulnerably blazing a trail as a nouveau feminist, guiding her readers about how to find inner strength to assertively live their own lives and prioritize their self-worth."

—**Andrea Colace**
Esq.

"Laura Melane's candid memoir, *Store Bought Baby*, is open, honest, authentic, and engaging. You'll be engrossed, intrigued, and informed."

—**Wendy McClellan**
Founder and CEO,
Structure for Success

"This beautiful book highlights the dichotomy of how love can be both sweet and salty. The author's story of repeatedly accepting inappropriate, even abusive, behavior from those she loved most is entirely relatable, as is the shame and self-doubt that comes with it. Laura Melane has a unique ability to share her story with grace, even when grace was not warranted."

—**Carla Engel**
Medical Capital Equipment Sales
and Contracting Specialist

Store Bought Baby

Store Bought Baby

A MEMOIR ABOUT ADOPTION, CODEPENDENCE, AND ESCAPING THE GOOD GIRL TRAP

LAURA MELANE

Store Bought Baby: A Memoir About Adoption, Codependence, and Escaping the Good Girl Trap

Copyright © 2025 by Laura Melane

First Published in the USA in 2025 by Peacock Proud Press, Phoenix, Arizona

ISBN 978-1-957232-23-2 Hardback
ISBN 978-1-957232-24-9 Paperback
ISBN 978-1-957232-25-6 eBook

Library of Congress Control Number: 2025902369

Editors
Laura L. Bush, PhD, peacockproud.com
Taryn Blanchard

Cover and Interior Design
Medlar Publishing Solutions Pvt Ltd., India

For my dad, Glenn,
who was a lifelong learner and loved books.
I miss you every day.

For my two sons.
I thought I knew what love was, and then I had you.
Love you both beyond.

For everyone
who needs and wants to heal.

Support Resources

for Adult Adoptees:
Adultadopteesupport.org
Adoption.com

for people worried about someone's drinking:
Al-Anon
Al-Anon.org

for those in abusive relationships:
National Domestic Hotline
www.thehotline.org
1-800-799-7233

Table of Contents

Part 2: Choosing Everyone Except Me

Part 3: Choosing Myself

Part 4: My Adoption Journey

Opening

I didn't know who I was

In 1969, a full-of-life airman named Glenn Alderman was working on a military airplane over Papua New Guinea. He was on his latest mission for the Air Force as part of an outfit that supported NASA, flying ground stations that communicated with astronauts in space. If all went to plan on the mission, and even if it didn't, it would be party time once they got back on the ground.

Meanwhile, back home in Florida, Glenn's wife Annette was trying everything she could to put a call through to the airplane he was on. The young married couple had been trying to start a family for several years, but they hadn't been able to conceive. Instead, they turned to adoption.

Finally, the call connected.

"Glenn!" Annette shouted over the noise of the airplane. "The baby is here, and I think I'm pregnant! What do we do?"

The Universe is a funny, fickle thing. Sometimes it throws you a curveball when you least expect it. As it turned out, the

Aldermans *could* get pregnant after all. But having two babies at the same time—one biological and one adopted—wasn't part of the plan. How would they make it work? Could they afford it financially?

Glenn could barely hear Annette. But, loud and clear, a voice deep inside him whispered, *Take that baby.*

"Take it! Take it! I love you, bye," he told Annette with the exuberance of a soon-to-be father riding high on endorphins and adrenaline.

In his excited rush, Glenn didn't even ask if their newly adopted baby was a boy or a girl. He just wanted the child.

And that's how Glenn and Annette Alderman, my adoptive parents, came to have one store bought baby and one home-grown baby.

A Journey of Adoption, Insecurity, and Family Dysfunction

My name is Laura, and I love getting lost in a book. The written word is a magical thing. Reading a book is like going on a journey. Like many kids, the imagination, characters, and worlds that can come alive in stories drove me to spend hours with my nose in the pages of books when I was young. As I got older, I shifted to reading books about personal growth, feminism, spirituality, health, and grief. Books have helped me overcome hard, persistent struggles that dogged me for years and become the person I'm meant to be.

When I was reflecting on the next journey I wanted to embark on as a fiftysomething divorced mother of two, as an adult child of adoption, as a "recovering codependent," and as a former business owner in the health and wellness space, authoring my own book was a no-brainer. I had an intuitive sense that it was the right time to share my deeply personal story, and that doing so might help someone else find an answer, a starting point, or a little bit of hope that could set them on their own journey of growth and healing.

For most of my life, I didn't know who I was. I was put up for adoption the day I was born. My adoptive mom Annette found out she was pregnant with my adoptive sister Heather the same month that she and Glenn officially took me in through a closed adoption. Heather is eight months and one day younger than me. We were peas and carrots in looks and personality, drastically different yet still the closest of sisters and friends. We almost shared a sort of telepathy with each other. She's the yin to my yang, and we haven't known life without each other.

When I was young, my adoptive mom once announced in her Southern Mississippi drawl—and with lots of love—that she had one "store bought baby" (me) and one "homegrown baby" (Heather). Today, because of her dementia, Mom can't remember saying this. To me, being her store bought baby is a badge of love and commitment from my entire adoptive family, as well as a badge of my own strength and resilience.

Being adopted left me with so many questions that neither I nor my adoptive parents could answer. They didn't hide anything from me as a child. As soon as I was old enough to understand, they told me the few facts they'd been told by the adoption attorney—that my birth mother was young when she had me, that she didn't have the means to take care of me, and that she wanted me to have a better life. While these details sound nice, I still felt a void that I couldn't fill. No matter how close I was with Heather, no matter how strongly I knew my parents wanted me, I experienced that void in a way that profoundly shaped who I was.

Unless you've been adopted, you can't understand. There's something missing. There's a void in your soul. For me, that void was even more pronounced for a few reasons.

First, throughout my childhood, I had a health condition that is passed down genetically from biological parent to child. Somewhere out there, I had birth parents who held the answers to my medical history, including which side of the family I inherited my health condition from, and I didn't have access to them. Every time I went for an appointment at a new dentist or doctor's office, I had to disclose that I didn't know my medical history. It frustrated me to no end, and it contributed to why I worked in health and wellness for my entire career, first as a nurse, then as the owner of my own business: Healing Soul Wellness & Fitness.

Second, growing up the adopted child of parents who also have their own biological daughter made me feel like I stuck out and didn't fit in. Heather was a carbon copy of our parents. The three of them had the same body type, and Heather was, in my young mind, much prettier than me. She was blonde, blue-eyed, tall, and skinny. I was short and had a stockier build, with dark hair and darker blue eyes that seemed plain at the time. I always envied Heather's long legs. Because of my insecurity about how I looked, as a teenager I kept the lights off in the bathroom so I didn't have to look at myself. Whenever I looked in the mirror, my flaws were all I saw. I didn't even submit a photo for my senior yearbook in high school because I didn't like any pictures of me. I've struggled with this my entire life.

In school, I was a grade ahead of Heather because of where our birthdays fell on the calendar. When friends and classmates found out we were sisters, they often got confused because we were so different from one another. They would ask questions ranging from benign curiosity to inappropriate—or there was awkward silence.

We want to stay where it's comfortable and familiar. We tell our-selves, *What if I change and it's worse?* But what we should be asking ourselves is, *What if I change and it's amazingly better and beyond my wildest dreams?* In the past, I've feared being on my own. Today, after much healing, I can honestly say I've made the changes I feared and that this is the best time of my life.

Movies and television shows have also begun to change. I love that there are more female writers and producers today, like Shonda Rhimes, Reese Witherspoon, and Greta Gerwig. One standout Shondaland TV show is *Bridgerton*, based on the book series by Julia Quinn. Set in an alternative London Regency era, it superbly addresses topics of racial, gender, and social class inequality. In a period when women existed to marry and were treated as property, whose strategic marriages could improve the status of their family, this show subverts and rebels against these norms and expectations. One of the lines in Season 3 struck me hard: "Ladies do not have dreams; they have husbands." It was not that long ago that this was the reality for the vast majority of women, and today women still experience forms of oppression and inequality that make this show poignant. *Bridgerton* highlights the oppression of women, then cleverly denounces it through stories of female empowerment.

It's time for girls and women everywhere to dream and make the lives they want a reality.

What you're reading right now is a memoir I've written about adoption and codependence, insecurity and dysfunction, and toxic behaviors and beliefs that trap good girls everywhere. My story is not about being a victim or bitter toward family or roman-tic partners. I don't see myself as a victim, and I don't hold any bitterness toward anyone who brought negativity into my life. There are no villains in my story. This memoir is about taking

useful lessons from the experiences I and so many women like me go through in our regular lives. It's about sharing the wisdom I've fought hard for so others might have an easier go of it.

To protect the privacy of loved ones, friends, and others, I have changed most names and some minor details throughout the memoir without altering any underlying lessons. This account of my life comes from my own perspective, which means the stories, interpretations, and reflections are filtered through my personal lens and view. It is, by its nature, subjective. My aim is to provide an authentic narrative that captures the essence of my journey, complete with the emotions, biases, and insights that have shaped my understanding of the world. While others may have different recollections or viewpoints, this memoir represents my truth as I have lived and perceived it.

Follow along with me on my journey searching for my biological parents and learning that I had a God-given family around me the entire time. Follow along with me on my journey to overcome the void that lived inside me for so long and the codependency that I carried into my romantic relationships. Follow along with me on my journey to stop trying so hard to be lovable, loved, and someone other people choose, so, instead, I could become someone who chooses myself, creates my own joy, and knows my own self-worth. Follow along with me as I discover my true identity, intuition, and voice. These are foundational parts of who we are as humans—that women in particular can be denied too often in our lives.

At the end of my book, I identify the top five books that have most influenced my journey. Consider whether they might be books for you to pick up too, or what books make your own "top five" list. This is a simple way to spark your inspiration, creativity, and commitment to your learning and growth. We all deserve so much in life, including life-enriching books.

I deserved so much more in life than what I settled for, and so do you. Whether you're in the middle of your own journey, right at the start of it, or not sure how to even start, I hope my story helps you choose yourself. Choosing yourself is an act of love. At the end of the day, we can't love others, and we can't love our lives, without first loving ourselves.

Choose you—every single day.

PART 1

Growing Up With Dysfunction

CHAPTER 1

Lost Innocence

I knew men liked to look at women

One summer, my sixteen-year-old cousin—let's call him Mitch—came to stay with my family in Washington. Both my parents worked, so they were gone during the day while Mitch babysat us for the summer. I was ten years old, and my sister Heather was almost ten.

Like many families, we often traveled to our relatives' homes at Thanksgiving and Christmas. During the holidays, I loved playing with Mitch and all my other cousins. I had nothing but positive feelings toward Mitch.

Soon after he arrived that summer, I saw Mitch watching something out the front window. Our home was in a cul-de-sac, so I quietly got myself in a position to see what he was looking at. Mitch was staring at my pretty sixteen-year-old neighbor, Helen. She was lying on a silver reflecting blanket in her front yard while she sunbathed in a green bikini.

The way Mitch looked at her made me feel uncomfortable.

I knew men liked to look at women. When we lived in Florida, my sister and I found my dad's *Playboy* magazines. We looked at them and laughed. My grandpa was visiting at the time and caught us, telling us not to look. The magazines soon disappeared from the bookcase. I learned at a young age that men wanted to look at women without their clothes on. I was just too young to know why.

One day Mitch got out of the shower and went to his room, but not before flashing his penis at me and Heather. We laughed, thinking it was funny, thinking he was just entertaining us. We were too young to know how to react to someone who was supposed to be caring for us and instead was being sexually inappropriate. We were probably afraid and confused underneath the laughing, but we played along with the game. In his room, Mitch lay on the bed naked with an erect penis and pretended to be asleep. Heather and I kept looking at him, laughing and whispering to each other.

That was the first penis I'd ever seen, except for when I saw a toddler in the neighborhood pull out his little penis and giggle as he peed all over Heather. I ran into the house, grossed out, telling my mom what had happened.

The next day and the day after that, Mitch exposed himself to us again and again, pretending to be asleep. Then he asked Heather to get on top of him.

"No," I told her. "Don't do that! That's how you get pregnant!"

I don't know how I'd learned how someone gets pregnant. It might have been from all the medical books my dad kept in the house, which I looked at often. I was always curious about bodies and where babies come from, especially since I was adopted. This curiosity may be one of the reasons I became a nurse.

When I stopped Heather from getting on top of Mitch, he seemed surprised—shocked even. He probably didn't know much about girls' anatomy or how people got pregnant. Most sixteen-year-olds then (and maybe now too) didn't know much about sex because their parents, like mine, didn't talk about sex with their children. I had to learn about male and female anatomy from medical books, whatever misinformation I picked up from friends, and Judy Blume books like *Are You There God? It's Me, Margaret*.

To my knowledge, Mitch didn't bother Heather again after that.

Later that day, he began chasing us both around the house. At some point, Heather stopped playing and disappeared. Mitch and I were alone in my parents' bedroom as he was tickling me on their bed, making me laugh. I was wearing terry cloth shorts, and suddenly, out of nowhere, Mitch pulled my shorts aside and rammed his finger inside me and pulled it out quickly.

Oh my gosh! my little mind thought. *What was that? What did he just do?*

The pain kicked in, and I started to cry. I ran to my room. Playing with my older cousin had gone from being a fun tickling game to something painful, frightening, and confusing. I may have had an idea of how babies were made, but I did not know about my own anatomy or understand what he had done.

I never told Heather. I never told my mom. I never told anyone.

Since I had laughed and been curious about bodies, I thought I would get in trouble, or that Mitch might get in trouble, and that I was to blame for what had happened.

Soon after that, my cousin went home.

"What happened to Mitch?" I asked Mom, trying to find out if he'd told her anything.

"He wanted to go home," she said.

Why did he want to go home? I wondered. *Was it because of me? Because of what happened?* I worried that I'd done something wrong, and someone might find out.

Here was my cousin that I really loved and had a great history with, but I had no way of knowing how to process why he'd hurt me like that. When he left, I felt relieved but still unsure about what had happened.

As I got older, I realized Mitch knew what he'd done was wrong. I also realized that his "play" had been grooming me and Heather to manipulate us, testing us to see what he could get from us and how far he could go before we might tell him to stop—or tell on him.

Maybe Mitch left because he felt guilty, or he didn't want to continue that behavior with us. Maybe someone had done this to him too, and he was mimicking their abuse. I can't know for sure, but I'm certain he knew it wasn't right.

This was the first traumatic experience I had in my life. After such a frightening and confusing encounter with Mitch, I began to hide any hurt I went through. This was the beginning of the repressing coping mechanism I would continue well into the future.

CHAPTER 2

A Father's Journey

I'm certain the Universe intervened

My Adoptive Dad, Glenn Alderman

My adoptive dad, Glenn Alderman, grew up having to take care of himself. He had two siblings: a little sister named Mae and a big brother named Dean. When they were all very young, their father Garrett Alderman left their mother to be with a woman named Merna. After the divorce, Merna didn't want Garrett to associate with his kids. My dad's mother Dot struggled to take care of three young kids by herself. She was uneducated and only made a little money cleaning homes and doing laundry. After Garrett left, Dot sent Dean to live with family members and Glenn to a boys' home (essentially an orphanage). She kept Mae, who was still a baby. My dad was visibly sad when he told this story, and I always felt sorry for him.

When I was in my forties, Dad told me a little about his time at the boys' home and the "den mother" who oversaw all the boys. I'm probably the only person he ever told anything about it.

"I hated her," he said. She had sexually abused him. I could see the hurt child and son inside my dad as he told me this. He felt like he'd been abandoned by his family. As a child, that was traumatic for him, and I think he knew it was a significant source of his pain when he got older.

"Yeah," he told me mechanically. "Dean went to live with family, Mae got to stay with Mom, and I got sent to a boys' home." After two years, Dean and Dad returned to live with Dot for the rest of their childhoods.

Because he only had himself to rely on, Dad grew up to become either fiercely independent or a loner, depending on how you frame it. He moved through the world on his own, even when family or friends were around him. Dad joined the Air Force at the age of eighteen. His job involved telemetry, the process of collecting and transmitting data from remote or inaccessible locations to a central location for analysis and monitoring. This is commonly done through the use of electronic devices and communication systems. He traveled the world extensively, even living in Japan for two years. Dad went up in airplanes and relayed information between astronauts in the space shuttles and NASA scientists on the ground. Pretty cool!

Dad also became an alcoholic, which placed a strain on his close relationships. He and my adoptive mother Annette Reagh married in 1967. They tried to have their own biological child but weren't successful. They adopted me in the winter of 1969. But that same month, Mom found out she was pregnant with Heather, who was born in the summer of 1970. They divorced in 1986 when Heather and I were sixteen years old.

Based on what I know about their relationship, Mom came to hold resentment toward Dad because he drank so much and, as a result, was often absent from our lives. She had to do everything at home while working full-time. Dad never even cooked dinner for us; his idea of cooking was opening a can of Beans and Weenies.

Mom still talks about it to this day. "He was unreliable. I'd call up at the bar, wanting him to come home, but he wouldn't. I could never rely on him to pick you up from school or sports."

At the age of sixty-nine, Dad got a DWI (Driving While Intoxicated). It was a wake-up call for him. He was mandated to get sober or go to jail. That's when he realized he had a problem and didn't drink for the rest of his life.

I think Dad had a very high IQ but very little common sense or people skills. As a child, you think your parents know everything. Then you grow up and realize your parents are only human. They experience their own traumas and limitations, which they may or may not ever change or heal from. This affects who they are and what they can bring to parenthood.

Here's an example of Dad's lack of common sense. One year I asked him to bring a cheese platter to our family Christmas party. Instead of putting it in his refrigerator after he bought it, he left it sitting out on his counter.

On the evening of the party when he brought it to my house, I thought, *What's wrong with this cheese? It looks weird.* I took a sniff. It had gone bad.

"Dad," I asked, "did you put the platter in the fridge when you bought it?"

"No," he admitted.

Needless to say, I didn't let anyone eat the cheese. It had never occurred to Dad that the platter needed to be refrigerated.

Similarly, when I opened my business, Healing Soul Wellness & Fitness, Dad had no concept of what being a business owner was like or how long it might take to start turning a profit. He was clueless.

"Yeah, Dad," I told him. "It typically takes three to five years to turn a profit."

"Really?" he asked. "I thought you'd be making a profit right away."

Dad had this naïveté and innocence about him that he never fully lost. He never remarried and lived alone. I tried to talk to him about where he might want to go should his health start to fail.

"I'll just go to Washington, DC," he replied. "They have a veterans place there."

"What's this place in DC?" I asked.

I don't think he knew.

"Suppose you had a stroke," I said. "You can't move, and you can't get to DC. What should we do?"

Dad just got angry. He had no plan and didn't know if or how his VA benefits worked. More than once, he told me he didn't want to talk about it anymore. Somehow, he thought the government would take care of it. He didn't make any arrangements for the possibility that something might happen to him—which it did, and it was a mess.

At eighty-six years old, Dad became ill right before Thanksgiving with what he thought was the flu. He was having trouble breathing. I was out of town, so Heather took him to the hospital. Doctors said he'd had a heart attack and was suffering from valley fever and pneumonia. He spent two weeks in the hospital before moving to a rehab facility for thirty days.

Then an administrator at the rehab facility told me, "He's getting better. He needs to leave."

"Are you kidding me?" I exclaimed. He wasn't getting better. As a former nurse, I knew he was dying.

"You weigh 180 pounds," a nurse reported to Dad while I was in the room with him.

No way! I thought. He had no appetite and had lost so much weight; that couldn't be accurate. Even Dad knew he didn't weigh that much.

"I can't get up," he said repeatedly. "I cannot get up." It wasn't that he didn't want to get up. The medical staff just wasn't getting it.

Someone on the staff finally weighed themselves and announced, "This scale is off."

They discovered that, at six feet, one inch, Dad weighed only 143 pounds. His heart was functioning at only 25 percent capacity. His body was wasting away.

I called my niece Stephanie, who had worked in assisted living and had contacts who could help find Dad a care facility, since he still needed medical care. She connected me with a woman named Brenda, who found a three-person group home in Mesa that would take Dad in. I would pay the costs out of pocket while going through the complicated process to get his VA benefits sorted out.

The day that Dad was supposed to go to the group home, he died alone in the rehab facility. I was working that morning. I planned to grab a quick lunch before heading to Dad so I could be there when they moved him to the group home that evening. After finishing with my last client, I checked my cell phone and saw a message to call the facility. The nurse I spoke to broke the news that Dad had died.

"He didn't want to eat breakfast this morning," the nurse said. "He told me he was going home."

Well, he went home. Dad had a habit of leaving our family parties without saying goodbye. He left this world with an Irish goodbye.

Tremendous sadness and guilt swamped me for not being there when he died.

I raced to the rehab facility, crying, calling my family on the way to let them know he had died. Heather burst into tears on the phone and told me she'd meet me at the facility.

The door to Dad's room was closed when I arrived. I walked in, prepared to see him. He was lying there peacefully. Throughout my nursing career, I saw the bodies of many people after they'd passed. But to see your parent lying there, knowing you will never be able to talk with him again—it's a devastating feeling. I held Dad's hand. I played his favorite song on my phone, "Rhapsody in Blue," and cried. Not only was the grief soul-crushing, but I was also in shock that he had died there alone.

To this day, I'm not happy with the way my dad's life ended. Months later, I shared with one of the rehab facility's head nurses that the nursing staff had told us Dad "was improving" and needed to be moved, when in reality, he'd been actively dying. I was pissed. Several people told me to sue the facility, but I was too deep in my grief to pursue it, and it wouldn't bring my dad back.

Dad got sick around Thanksgiving 2022 and died on January 13, 2023. In his final weeks, I said what I needed to say to him. I told him I loved him and thanked him for being my dad.

"Hey," I joked, "when you get to the other side, would you send me some nice guy, please?"

"Oh, sure, sure," he retorted. His mind was still sharp, despite the exhaustion caused by his failing heart. I was in awe that his mind was still intact.

Dad believed in an afterlife. He said he wasn't afraid to die. I think when we pass, we're going to be enveloped in so much love.

"You'll get to see your parents and brother," I told him.

Dad was at peace with it. He knew his body was giving out. There was no way he'd want to live like that. He was still independent and driving until he went into the hospital in November 2022. After going through so much in his life and growing with such commitment once he decided to get sober, he knew he had lived a good life. It was time to "go home."

Even though my dad had his struggles, he taught me many things. One of his favorite sayings was "patience is a virtue." He modeled patience for me. He also taught me to love books and movies, and to stick up for the underdogs in life. I miss him every day.

Glenn's DWI and Journey to Sobriety

In December 2004, Dad was living in Washington state. He wanted to visit me and Heather, who had both moved to Arizona by then. Chad, my husband at the time, wanted us to visit his parents in Washington for Christmas. (Chad is also from Washington state, but we met in Arizona.) Chad and I decided he would take our sons Westin and Wyatt to see his family before Christmas, then come home before Christmas Day. My dad would fly down while they were gone and spend time with me and Heather, staying to celebrate Christmas Day with all of us.

During Dad's visit, he and I went to a Christmas party at a friend's house. She and I attended the same church for many years. Every December, she and her family hosted a Christmas party at her home, and her husband set up an elaborate Christmas train set. I knew Dad would love to see it; he'd loved trains as a kid and always wanted a train set.

We went to the party and enjoyed ourselves. We came home, and I put on *Elf*, one of my favorite Christmas movies, since it was still early in the evening. We watched the movie in the living room, but Dad kept going into the kitchen. I wasn't sure what he was doing until he ended up "falling asleep" on the couch. I tried to wake him but ended up leaving him where he was. We were living in a two-story condo at the time while the house we planned to move into was being built. The guestroom and the boys' shared room were upstairs. The master bedroom was on the first floor, where I went to bed.

At one o'clock in the morning, a loud crash woke me. I opened my bedroom door to find Dad standing there, confused, with blood running down his lower face and vomit all over the floor. He had fallen and hit his nose. He was obviously drunk and could hardly stand up. I got him over to a chair and cleaned him up as best I could. Then I helped him upstairs to his bed and prayed he didn't wake up again.

Downstairs, I cleaned up the vomit. As I did this, I started to feel angry—as well as very concerned about Dad's drinking. I went into the kitchen and finally noticed a nearly empty bottle of whiskey that we'd had for years but never drank. I didn't sleep at all for the rest of the night. I was listening to make sure Dad didn't get up or fall down the stairs. I was angry and worried at the same time.

The next day, I called Heather and told her what had happened. She came over, and we tried to talk with Dad about his drinking. He seemed sad and didn't say much.

Eventually, I told him, "You can't drink anymore while you're staying here, okay?"

A few nights later, we went to another Christmas party, and he didn't drink. It felt awkward with other people drinking around us, but maybe I was just hyperaware of it. We ate, then left early.

Once Chad and the boys got home, we didn't talk about it anymore. After celebrating Christmas together, Dad returned to Washington state. Heather called him in early January and offered some information on Alcoholics Anonymous (AA) meetings in his area.

I called after she spoke to him. "Did you look into any of the AA meetings Heather gave you?"

Dad became very angry, very fast. "If you're going to call and bring this up, then don't call me at all." He hung up on me. Dad had never hung up on me before.

Shocked, I was really worried about him.

He's going to kill himself or someone else while drinking and driving, I thought. I knew how often he went to bars, and that he must be driving home drunk.

I prayed. I didn't know what kind of relationship I would have with Dad moving forward. I didn't know if he would speak to me or take my phone calls. I prayed that God would protect and help him. He lived so far away and was clearly in denial. I felt powerless to help him.

I may never speak to my dad again, I thought suddenly, going cold. And there'd be little I could do about it. All I could do was surrender it to a higher power to protect him and other people.

About a week later, on January 20, 2005, Dad called me. He'd been arrested for an extreme DWI the night before. Dad was given two options: He could either go to jail or go to AA and have an ignition interlock device installed in his car for a year. Thankfully, he chose the second option.

"You know," he told me after, "the policewoman who pulled me over was an angel."

That night, instead of walking to his local bar, he'd decided to drive. On his way home, the police officer saw him pull out of the bar and followed him to his apartment complex. He was wasted, and she arrested him. He doesn't remember much about that night, only what she told him. Dad had never been arrested before. While I'm sure he had driven drunk many, many times, he had never gotten caught. He was a law-abiding military man who followed all the rules in other areas of his life. This made a huge impact on him and finally got him to recognize his problem with alcohol.

The officer, the arrest, and AA saved Dad's life.

He went to AA meetings regularly and quit smoking at the same time. He lived another seventeen years sober. He got to see his four grandkids grow up, and he made amends with me. I got to know my dad sober. We talked more than we ever had, even before the debacle at Christmas in 2004. He opened up more to me about his childhood, his alcoholism, and everything and anything else. It felt like I was getting to know someone familiar, yet also completely new. In 2010, Dad moved from Washington to Arizona to be closer to me and Heather. Beginning in 2016, I even talked to him openly about my separation and divorce from Chad. Those conversations meant everything to me. We enjoyed going to movies and talking about books together, having lunch or dinner, and attending my sons' sporting events whenever he was able to.

Dad also gave back by tutoring kids in math and reading. He loved helping them. He could get feisty when talking about politics and loved to debate how he was right. Mostly, though, he was a gentle soul. He told me, even after seventeen years, that he would still dream about alcohol. But he never drank again.

I'm certain the Universe—God, the Source, the Divine, whatever you want to call it—intervened. My prayer for help was heard and answered. I was in awe of how quickly it happened. Ask and ye shall receive. My father's alcoholism played a starring role in the dysfunctional family dynamics I experienced as a child. I don't blame him for it, though. He was a product of his own hardship-filled upbringing. He was a child of divorce, he went on to have a marriage that ended in divorce, and then I went on to have a marriage that ended in divorce too. Dad's trauma led to a lifelong battle with addiction that affected all his close relationships. As you'll read in Part 2, I went on to marry a man who also battled addiction.

Together, my dad and I are part of the same story of a family's generational trauma. Trauma can be transmitted intergenerationally through learned behaviors, coping mechanisms, and family dynamics. It's often shaped by the cultural and social context in which it occurs, like the church communities we were always part of that set norms all across America for attitudes, behaviors, and what was and wasn't talked about openly. Much of my dad's life was filled with silence, and right up until his DWI, he was committed to silencing anyone who might help him.

But my dad didn't only live a life of addiction and silence. He also lived a life of resilience and recovery. The growth he fought for in his later years helped me grow. It was proof that anyone can choose to make significant lifestyle changes, no matter their age or life stage. The power of transformation lies in all of us. That means it's up to each of us to transform ourselves, building our strength from within and drawing on the support of those around us. Once Dad made the choice to change, he accepted support from AA, me, and my sister Heather. I'm eternally grateful.

When my dad went through his AA recovery program, he wrote a letter about his drinking. We found it in his belongings after his death. I know in my heart my dad would want me to share this letter, exactly as he wrote it, if it could help someone else.

I started drinking when I was in high school. One of the guys in our gang had a false ID and would buy the beer. We'd all get drunk and then get sick—that's what a 16-year-old does.

After high school, I joined the Air Force. In the service, if you didn't drink, there was something wrong with you. My first duty station was in Japan. I drank sake, akadama (Japanese plum wine), Japanese beer, and whiskey. Every weekend was party time. I really loved it. There was always booze and women galore. I was in seventh heaven.

There was no such thing as being underage. I was 18 when I got to Japan and just turned 21 when I got back to the States, so I never had any problems with that. When I got back to the States, I was stationed in Sioux City, Iowa, where I continued to party. We used to go over to South Dakota, which was just across the bridge, and if you were able to see over the bar, you could get a drink.

I got my discharge from the Air Force in Sioux City. I had a fairly new car. On the way home to Eugene, Oregon, by way of Dallas, Texas, I wrecked my car. I was drunk at the time, but the cop didn't give me a ticket. I still had my Air Force I.D., and in Texas in 1958, that was like a free pass.

When I got home after a lot of stuff going on, I received a bill from the State of Texas for $200.00. It might as well have been for a million. I didn't have it. The Air Force recruiter kept coming around—and offered me $500.00 to reenlist. So I reenlisted.

I paid the $200.00 to Texas, and with the remaining $300.00 I partied with all my old buddies in Eugene. I blew the whole thing on booze and good times.

Then I went to McChord AFB. I was broke. I spent five years at McChord and only drank on the weekends. In 1963, I got stationed at Charleston, South Carolina. While I was there, I went on Project Deep Freeze at the Antarctic.

We flew out of Christchurch, New Zealand. In November of 1963, President Kennedy was shot, and because of my accent and possibly my clothes, I couldn't buy a beer in town because all the Kiwis (that's what New Zealanders called themselves) felt sorry for me, or any Yank. I really milked that!

Anyway, after South Carolina, I went to Tech School in Denver and then to Patrick AFB Florida. I was in an outfit called ARIA. We supported NASA. We were flying ground stations for telemetry and radio communications with the astronauts. This was really great because we literally went all over the world. If we had a successful mission, it was Partee Time! Even if we didn't have a successful mission, we partied anyhow.

In retrospect, I really don't think I was an alcoholic at that time because I really believe I was a social drinker. I never drank alone. Ever.

While I was at Patrick, we had one mission where we went to the Fijis. We met this Fijian chief and went up to his village. We all sat in a big circle and drank kava. I had never tried it before. It made my face numb. I was told that if we had drank a lot more, we would get numb all over. Oh well, I preferred beer and/or whiskey.

When I retired from the Air Force, I came back home to the Northwest. By this time, I had a wife and two children. I went to work for Boeing in 1978. I think this is when my drinking started to change. Almost every day after work, I stopped at the Golden Steer and got slightly drunk. I did this until 1986, when

I moved out. My wife said it was the booze or her. Guess which one I picked?

My two girls were in high school, and I really missed them. But the thing was, I only moved down the street, so I saw them all the time.

Then I retired from Boeing in 1993. That's when, I believe, the drinking got serious. Every two or three days without exception, I got drunk. I also started getting sick on occasion, something I hadn't done in 20 years. To fast forward to 2005, I was getting blackouts. In December of 2004, I was staying with my oldest daughter in Arizona and I blacked out—twice—on two different occasions. My daughter became quite concerned and told me what I had done. She said I should get help. I got mad. I told her to more or less mind her own business. I could take care of myself.

Then, on Jan. 19, 2005, the hammer fell. I got pulled over on a DWI. I really don't remember much about that night because I was in my usual condition—wasted. But I remember everything since then—1/19/05, my AA birthday, because that's the last time I had a drink or will ever have a drink.

CHAPTER 3

A Near Miss and Open Communication

I tried to do better

My dad worked as an engineering technician at Boeing with a man named Bill, who became a family friend for a few years. He was tall and slim, had dark thinning hair, and wore glasses. Mom, Dad, Heather, and I all had fun at his wedding, where he married a woman who already had two little girls. They were younger than me and Heather and so cute. They made adorable flower girls during the ceremony.

I didn't know his wife and stepdaughters until we went to the wedding. Bill had always come to our house by himself. After he got married, he never came over again.

Bill was a photographer and always had a camera on him. It was part of his identity. Back then, everyone still used cameras with film, not smartphones. A couple times, he took photos of me and my sister when we were around ten or eleven years old.

Both Heather and I were gymnasts, so one time he photographed us doing flips and gymnastics poses in the living room. Another time, he snapped a photo of our whole family at Christmas. During that photo session, he also took separate pictures of me and Heather, including a sweet one with me where I held up a wreath in front of my face like a frame.

It all seemed natural, innocent, and spontaneous. Bill shared the photos with us, and my mom put them in a photo album.

"You guys can come over to my house any time you want," he said once, offhandedly, to all of us. We never did.

One day in high school, Mom was driving me home from gymnastics practice. She told me that Bill had been convicted of molesting his stepdaughters. He went to prison.

I felt nauseous. Bill had seemed like a nice man.

Oh my god, I thought. *This guy is a creep!*

Why are there so many men who hurt little girls?

The fact that he could have been using these innocent pictures of us or other kids having fun for any reason other than capturing a family memory for us grossed me out. It made me feel like Heather and I had had a near miss—like bullets just missing our heads. I dug out the photos he'd given me and tore them up.

I think my mom had some protective instinct that kept her from letting us visit Bill's house. She put up that boundary, even if she didn't know why. This "near miss" also reminds me of the risks that stepchildren, children of adoption, and sadly, *all* children face in their own homes where they're supposed to be safest. I was supposed to be safe at home with my cousin Mitch too.

It breaks my heart. These stories of trauma, of nauseating near misses, of systemic risks and failures in adoption and child protective services need to be told. The horrifying experiences that so many children endure, even when they aren't adopted, can thwart their dreams when they grow up. These experiences lead to any number of harmful and destructive behaviors as adults. Take your pick. My own unhealthy, codependent, abusive relationships with men, which I discuss in Part 2, are deeply entangled with my experience and identity as a child of adoption. Just as important, the men in my life also endured their own terrible childhood experiences. The consequences don't go away, even when we survive them.

According to Rape, Abuse & Incest National Network (RAINN), 93 percent of child sexual abuse is perpetrated by persons known to the victim. One in nine girls and one in twenty boys under age eighteen experience sexual abuse or assault.

All I remember about Mom sharing that Bill had abused his stepdaughters were the facts. I don't remember ever talking about Bill with my dad, and my mom didn't say anything else about what happened to those two children or express any opinion. She probably thought, *How sad for those little girls.* She kept it to herself, though.

Maybe Mom didn't elaborate or react to purposely *not* upset me. But why would she tell me he was incarcerated for molesting his stepdaughters at all? Mom wasn't one to talk about difficult things like that. For example, when Heather and I were entering puberty, all she did was hand me a box of pads and a book.

"Here, read this," she said, assuming Heather and I could figure out getting our first period on our own. She also gave me a pamphlet about sex, but she didn't talk with me about the information at all. Back then, people like my mom didn't talk about sex or bodies.

I tried to do better when I had Westin and Wyatt.

As a parent, it's hard not to look back and wish I had done some things differently, but I had the best intentions. I believed birth control should be everybody's responsibility, so I made sure my sons had books about their maturing bodies and talked to them about the changes they'd go through, and that those changes were normal. I know I could have done a better job at this. One thing I wish I would have done, which I didn't even think about at the time, was to educate my boys about female anatomy—what a period is, why women have them, how a woman gets pregnant— the actual chemistry of it. I don't know why I didn't do that. I was a nurse, after all. I think many men (and women, for that matter) do not understand menstrual cycles or their own hormones and how they affect you greatly throughout your entire life. To me, it's important to have knowledge about yourself, physically and mentally.

I modeled a healthy lifestyle for Westin and Wyatt by exercising and eating well. They would ask why all the food in our house had to be organic or why I bought healthier alternatives to chips when all they wanted were Doritos. I didn't ban unhealthy foods, but I made sure the majority of what we ate for meals and snacks in our home was nourishing for us.

Today my sons still call me when they're injured or sick, like when Westin crashed on a motorbike. He told me in some detail how he'd washed and bandaged the wound.

"That sounds great, Westin," I said. Then I went over to look at it. His injury was healing well, so I told him, "You're doing all the right things." I think my sons are probably more aware of how to take care of their health than other young men because of what I've taught them as a nurse. When they get sick, they know to take their temperature and increase fluids. They also know to be aware of any unusual changes in their bodies that might need medical attention.

When they were growing up, I also talked openly about the dangers of drugs and alcohol, as well as drinking and driving. I did not want them to develop drug and alcohol problems that seemed to be so prevalent on both sides of our family, including in our own home. I tried to shield them from the alcoholism taking place in our home, which I talk about in Part 3.

Raising boys right is essential to *not* creating men who become predators, abusers, or, more often, just don't understand when their behavior is toxic. Parental missteps and misinformation are a part of life that we all have to deal with, regardless of age, either as parents or as children. But missteps and misinformation can quickly be compounded by other negative effects of things like adoption, religion, and mental illness. When boys grow up to respect women and know how their behavior affects the people around them, fewer girls and women find themselves stuck in the "good girl" trap with no escape.

CHAPTER 4

Between Mothers, Daughters, and Sisters

I saw and felt it all

My Adoptive Mom Annette Reagh

My adoptive mom Annette Reagh was a force to be reckoned with. She coined the affectionate terms "store bought baby" and "homegrown baby" for me and my sister Heather, and I wear mine proudly. During my childhood, she was my main caregiver, and I was her daughter, just as Heather was.

Mom was an extroverted taskmaster. She was organized, structured, and a big planner. She took on too much and did much more than her fair share in running the household. How could she not when she was fundamentally a responsible person, while her husband was an alcoholic and absent father? Mom cooked, cleaned, and worked a full-time job as a junior high math teacher until I was eight years old. Then, when we moved to Kent,

Washington, she became a computer programmer for Boeing. She drove me to all my sports practices and did the hundreds of other unacknowledged things that mothers do every day.

Mom and I are similar, except I'm an introvert. Like her, I've always taken on too much in my relationships. I've always done more than my fair share. Unfortunately, I was married to an alcoholic, just like her. Both of us struggled with husbands who were physically and emotionally absent.

When I was a child, I didn't know my dad was an alcoholic. He was a calm, patient person. I can only remember two or three times when he ever got upset. But he was also disconnected and showed little interest in spending time with his family. While Dad would respond to me if I went to him, he wasn't forthcoming on his own and didn't take any initiative to engage with us. Even when he did take us places, like the Science Center, the movies, or a bookstore, there was always a distance that couldn't be crossed.

Intuitively, I knew something was wrong. Dad slept often, and I didn't understand why. When we lived in Florida, our house had a windowless interior room with a comfy brown La-Z-Boy in it. Dad would put on his big headphones, listen to music, and sleep in that chair for hours. Something didn't seem right about it, but I didn't know what.

Maybe all dads sleep a lot, I thought as a young girl. *Maybe he's tired a lot. Maybe he just wants to be alone.*

Dad slept so much because he was hungover frequently. He recovered from binges in that chair. It's a strange thing, having a father in your life, living with you and taking you places, yet not really talking or engaging with you in any meaningful way. He wasn't interactive, and he seemed to be lost in his own head often. Dad was a chronic avoider; he probably didn't even realize how much he was avoiding. As a child, I would never have been able to describe my dad's behavior like this. But now, as an adult and mother, I've seen fathers who are present, engaged, and active participants in their children's lives.

Wow, I think wistfully sometimes. *What would my life have been like if I'd had that kind of father?*

Dad didn't interact with my mom either. He went off and did his own thing. He would rather go out drinking. I didn't realize it at the time, but I rarely saw Dad with a smile on his face unless he was tipsy. Drinking made him happy. He used alcohol to numb the pain from the trauma he experienced in his own childhood. Mom didn't drink at all, having never liked the taste of alcohol, so it wasn't like she gave him the impression at the start of their relationship that she was interested in that type of lifestyle.

Recently, Mom told me, "When your dad and I started dating and first got married, I rarely saw him drink or smoke." He didn't overdo any of that around her. When he was in the Air Force, she accepted that he drank and partied with his military buddies. Like me, Mom married a man without truly knowing how important drinking and partying were to him.

Despite all this, Heather and I were loved. We had a roof over our heads, food in our bellies, and clothes on our backs. We didn't want for any of our basic needs. We had good lives. But there was little emotional connection in our house. Mom focused on the pragmatic tasks of running a household. While she would talk anyone and everyone's ear off, as a family we never talked about tough life subjects. Even when she told me about Bill the photographer, she didn't help me process it. She dropped the bare facts on me and left it at that. Those types of conversations often determine whether a young person grows up emotionally healthy or stunted.

Several years ago, Mom and I were having lunch at a local restaurant. I knew Susan, the owner, and she dropped by our table to catch up and chat about how everyone was doing.

Susan and I both had teenagers at the time and were discussing the challenges of life with them. Mom often didn't have much of a filter before she spoke. Out of the blue, she blurted out, "Yeah, one time, when you were a teenager, you said you wanted to kill yourself."

I was shocked and embarrassed. *Yikes, super inappropriate, Mom! Not the right time to say this in front of someone else.*

Susan probably thought, *What the hell?*

"Okay," I replied, then redirected the conversation.

As a teenager, I *did* have a tough time and probably had undiagnosed depression from a combination of struggling with being adopted, our family dysfunction, and normal adolescent hormonal changes. But I don't remember having suicidal thoughts or saying I did. I was a great student, active in sports, had fun with friends, and didn't exhibit signs of severe depression. I'd describe myself as having a sense of melancholy, which, looking back, was to be expected with the family dynamics I was navigating. I'm sure I was staying busy and over-functioning to avoid my problems at home.

Although Mom often said unfiltered things to or around other people, in our household, topics like suicide weren't even acknowledged or addressed when Heather and I were growing up. The filter inside our house was extremely strong. It wasn't a lack of love or caring. The problems that Mom and Dad had, as individuals and as parents, made them emotionally unavailable. We were also living in a society where many people found it impossible to talk about difficult issues like mental health, abuse, addiction, marriage struggles, and trauma.

Mom didn't know how to handle my teenage struggles, so she didn't. She didn't know how to handle Dad's drinking, so she didn't. According to Mom, she didn't say anything when Dad decided to move out during the summer of 1986, despite it taking him a couple months to find an apartment. She doesn't know why she didn't say anything. She never spoke to Dad about his alcoholism or what she needed (and wasn't getting) from him in their marriage. In the sobriety letter Dad wrote for AA, which we found after he passed away, he said Mom gave him an ultimatum: quit drinking or move out. Mom doesn't remember ever telling him that.

Whoever remembered it correctly, it's clear they had a dysfunctional relationship. As part of his AA recovery, Dad apologized and made amends to me for his drinking. He never did the same for Mom. I always hoped they might have a conversation or find some closure together, but she didn't want to see him. To this day, Mom still says, "When your dad left me . . ." I've tried so many times to get her to believe that he did her a huge favor by leaving. He was a full-on alcoholic and did not think rationally. All he really cared about was alcohol.

Without meaning to, Mom modeled for me the experience of a woman living in a situation she didn't like—but staying in it anyway. I grew up to repeat some of what had been modeled for me. As a child watching my parents, I also came to believe that life was just kind of . . . miserable. You grit your teeth and get through it. There wasn't much joy in our household. That didn't change until after the divorce when Mom met Harlan, who would become her second husband and my stepdad. Then, when Harlan died years later, joy left Mom again.

I want to have joy regardless of who is in my life. I want to be able to bring myself joy, instead of relying on someone else to do it for me.

My mom has taught me many things that I'm grateful for, like how to show up for those I love, how to be dependable and reliable, and how to help those in need. When I was in elementary school, she helped a refugee family from Cambodia adjust to America and brought them food and toiletries. I'll never forget that experience. She modeled how to be a well-educated woman. As a mother, she was always fair and never treated me or Heather differently. She always celebrated our birthdays and holidays in a big way. She was and is a thoughtful, kind person.

Today Mom has dementia. It's at a stage where she often knows that she doesn't know. She knows she's missing pieces of herself and her loved ones. Toward the end of finishing this book, my sister and I had to move her into a memory care facility. It's a sobering reality of the preciousness of life, and I treasure the moments I can spend with her. She still knows who I am luckily, but I know that may change in the future.

Most Sundays, I take Mom out to lunch to spend time with her and provide her with a change in her facility food. She's always loved to go out to eat. Not being fond of cooking, Mom has said over the years that her favorite thing to make is reservations. During many of our Sunday conversations, she's told me, "I can't remember anything anymore. I sure hope this doesn't happen to you. It's awful not to remember."

It's equally heartbreaking to see an intelligent, independent, responsible woman lose herself and have to depend on others to take care of her. Despite this, Mom has also come a long way. She's much more likely to make funny jokes or talk about tough topics that were complete "no-go zones" in our household when Heather and I were growing up, like my dad's drinking. She's more open than she used to be.

As Mom has gotten older, come to need help, and gone through some personal growth herself, our relationship has shifted. My perspective about our relationship has also shifted. I love my mom. She's not perfect. Comparatively speaking, though, I lucked out. I'm not perfect either, and I've come to appreciate her for what she provided me.

Mom doesn't drive anymore. This past Thanksgiving, she thanked me for driving her to and from dinner. "Well, look at it this way," I said. "You drove me everywhere I needed to be for the first sixteen years of my life until I got my license. Now, this is payback. I've got a lot of years to make up."

I do everything I can to take care of Mom in her elder years. I don't do it out of a sense of obligation. I do it out of love. I think there must be a divine reason she and I are both single at the same time. We've grown closer over the past few years because of this—a gift in light of both our losses. I might be her "store bought baby," but the care we've given each other at different times in our lives is reciprocal and mutual.

My Adoptive Sister Heather

I've never known life without my adoptive sister Heather, and she's never known life without me. I think of her as a ray of sunshine that lights up a room when she enters.

Heather is tall, skinny, and extroverted. I'm shorter and introverted. She has light-blue eyes and blonde hair. I have gray-blue eyes and dark-brown hair. Both our physical features and personalities are yin and yang. Yet as children, we were so in sync—almost like twins since we were less than a year apart in age. When we were young, my mom would dress us in matching clothes. People often asked if we were twins. My aunt Mae referred to us as *Snow-White and Rose-Red*, the Grimms' Fairy Tale about two sisters, one a quiet brunette and one an adventurous blonde. My parents had photos of Heather and I roughly at the same ages hung above their bed. In every picture Heather has a big smile on her face, or her mouth is open. I only have a smile in one. I was much more serious and pensive than Heather, even as a child. Where she was the talkative one, I was the listener.

33

She had many, many friends, and I had just a few close friends. We've always been very different, but still close sisters.

Whenever we played Pictionary and teamed up, we were unbeatable. We always complemented each other and always got each other, despite our differences. And, of course, the mutual experience of growing up in the same household often bonds siblings, whether they're related by blood or not. Nature and nurture are complicated.

When Heather and I were in high school, Dad sat us down and told us he was moving out.

"Do we have to move out too?" I asked. I wanted to know if we would have to change our entire lives.

"No," Dad replied. "You're going to stay here with your mom."

I got up, angry, and went to my bedroom. I didn't understand why Dad couldn't be a partner to Mom. I didn't know what was wrong with him, or why he acted so distant and removed—physically and emotionally—from us. We were his family, but he just floated through our lives. It was like living with a ghost. He was there, but he wasn't.

Soon, though, I felt relieved. Mom and Dad didn't really have a marriage. He was not a partner to Mom at all, and she was miserable. I didn't know why, but I saw and felt it all. After Dad announced he was moving out, I began to hope that it could be good for Mom. She deserved to be happy.

When Heather and I had dinner recently, I told her a bit about the writing I was doing for this book, mentioning some of the stories from our childhood. I wanted to get her thoughts and feelings about our family experiences.

"I always knew there was something wrong with Dad," I said.

"Oh, I had no clue," Heather replied. She was completely unaware of any problem. "You were always more sensitive to what was going on in the house than I was."

I know kids, in general, have different experiences of family life, even when they're raised in the same household. It's possible that Heather's inattentiveness was a defense mechanism she subconsciously used to protect herself against any family dysfunction related to Dad's alcoholism.

Families who go through struggles with alcoholism often keep secrets—from themselves, from each other, and from the outside world. Many families do everything they can to avoid looking at the problem, let alone talking about it or dealing with it. This also extends to other struggles that family members go through, like sexual abuse.

I never told Mom, Dad, or Heather about what happened with my cousin Mitch as a child. I didn't feel comfortable doing so. I thought I was to blame and would get in trouble. Dad contributed to the code of silence within our family simply by being absent all the time. While Mom was present and involved, she always had a bit of a judgmental side.

When we were teenagers, Mom was often impatient and bossy. Maybe that was because she was trying so hard to hold everything together. She had to parent us and work a full-time job without support from Dad. It makes sense that she'd be mad, resentful, hurt, and hurtful.

As a young person, I didn't want to add to Mom's burden or disappoint her. I always did what Mom told me. I was afraid of upsetting her.

If I do everything right and please her, I thought, *I won't add to her stress.*

Looking back, my mom was hard on my sister. Heather feels like she was more critical of her, and it damaged their relationship. I saw their conflict and felt sad for my sister. As a child, I could do nothing about it but shrink myself and stay quiet. I feel this contributed to me people pleasing to keep the peace.

35

Unlike me, Heather would challenge Mom, talk back more often, and do more of what she wanted. She wasn't rebellious or trying to act out on purpose; she was just a free spirit who couldn't be pinned down for long.

Mom was always responsible when it came to money. We weren't poor—Mom and Dad had good jobs—but they both grew up in poor households and internalized the scarcity mindset (especially my mom) that comes with that type of upbringing. I was always cautious with my money and spending.

I saved my money, and Heather spent hers. Heather would eat her Halloween candy all at once, and I'd still have mine at Easter. She loved to buy vinyl records, and Mom would comment disapprovingly on it regularly. Still, Heather enjoyed what she bought. Ultimately, I think Heather has been happier in life because she didn't worry so much and just enjoyed herself.

Mom's upbringing and scarcity mindset went hand in hand with her insistence that we get strong educations so we could support ourselves. I feel fortunate that those values about saving money and taking my education seriously were ingrained in me. Not going to college was never an option. College was something that automatically came after high school. Going to college was also a privilege. I know my parents saved specifically for me and my sister to do so. They paid for all of it, and I'm extremely grateful to them. Initially, Heather didn't want to go to college at all, but Mom put her foot down.

"You're going," she told Heather. "And that's that."

I don't see the bossy, impatient part of Mom as much anymore, especially now that she has dementia. Heather still does. Recently, Heather and I were with Mom when her bossiness came out.

"That needs to be done right now!" Mom snapped, surprising me.

Mom and Heather are both extroverted and like to talk. They'll talk to everybody and anybody about anything. That similarity means they can rub each other the wrong way. As an introvert, I'm more laid-back than Heather in responding to Mom. I sit back and think about what I'm going to say before I say it. I have been working on making sure I am honest about my feelings and not holding back or filtering my truth. I'm getting better at this.

The Bonds That Connect Family

My adoptive mom and sister have been two of the most influential women in my life. Relationships between mothers and daughters, and between sisters, can be complicated. I haven't always understood my mom, and we've had our ups and downs over the years. As Heather and I grew up and started families of our own, we didn't share as much about our lives. That pseudo-twin sense of being in sync faded, but we developed an adult relationship that's just as meaningful to me.

Being a woman in this world is hard. Bonds of motherhood and sisterhood, even when they're more passive than active, can keep us afloat when we feel like we're drowning in a society that still privileges male power over all else. These bonds are some of the most profound and intricate relationships we experience in life. They are woven together by threads of shared history, mutual support, unspoken emotion, and—if we're lucky—understanding. These relationships help shape us, mold our identities, and influence our worldviews in ways that are both beautiful and challenging.

In our household growing up, Heather and I didn't always get the emotional support we needed. Neither of our parents was nurturing, although obviously society taught us Mom was expected to be nurturing in a way that Dad wasn't. When we got home from school, it was up to me and Heather to get our homework done without prompting. We also had to entertain ourselves without our parents' involvement. We were latchkey kids of the eighties when both parents worked and kids like us had to fend for ourselves. When Mom wasn't at work or focused on the practicalities of running the household, she kept herself busy in other ways—likely so she didn't have to acknowledge the dysfunction taking place because of Dad's drinking. She was the team mom for my gymnastics team. She volunteered with the church. She always had something else going on. Today I understand this; I did the exact same thing to deal with the dysfunction in my own marriage.

So, while Heather and I had all our basic needs taken care of, not all our emotional needs were met. When I grew up, I developed unhealthy codependent relationships with my romantic partners because I thought they would give me the emotional support and validation I needed. Codependency is a psychological condition or behavioral pattern where someone excessively relies on others for their sense of self-worth, identity, and validation. In codependent relationships, one person may prioritize the needs and desires of another person to the extent that they neglect their own well-being. This can lead to a lack of boundaries, difficulty expressing their own emotions and needs, and an unhealthy sense of responsibility for others. Codependency often involves enabling behaviors, where one person consistently supports or enables the destructive behaviors of another, such as addiction or other self-destructive habits.

I look back on my own parenting and wonder if I could have been more emotionally supportive and present. I think I did better than my parents. I know I communicated better than them about some tough topics, and I tried to make sure my sons knew they could talk to me about anything. But I also know that I was frequently exhausted, just like Mom was during my childhood. I can only hope that if and when they have children of their own one day, Wyatt and Westin do better than both me and my parents. I also hope that the bond between them, as brothers, remains strong and that they help each other through life's challenges and losses.

PART 2

Choosing Everyone Except Me

CHAPTER 5

Seeds of Codependency

I stuck my head in the sand

Dating John and Feeling Like I Belonged

John was the first guy I dated right after high school. He had light-brown hair, green eyes, and freckles. I loved his wide, toothy grin and how often he showed it. Always smiling and laughing, John gave great hugs. He'd hug me at his house, around his family, after dinner, saying hello or goodbye, and just because he was happy and wanted to. His warmth and friendliness were so different from my own household.

My family members weren't touchy-feely with each other. My dad, in particular, was a passive and aloof man (when he was sober, at least). If I hugged him, he'd hug me back, but he never initiated a hug himself. When I was an adult, sometimes Dad would leave family gatherings without saying goodbye. Today I make a point of greeting my own sons with hugs just because I'm happy to see them, and I always say goodbye before leaving.

At the time, having John's open affection almost startled me. It was unfamiliar. I felt safe in his arms. He had a stocky, muscular build, and throughout my life, I've tended to be attracted to shorter men. I'm fairly stocky as well, whereas my adoptive family all had taller, leaner builds. Subconsciously, I must have wanted to see my own appearance reflected in the people I had romantic relationships with.

John and I met in high school through overlapping friend groups, but we didn't begin dating until right after I graduated. We were together for two years, from 1987 to 1989. During that time, I went away for my first year of college at Western Washington University, then did my second year back home at community college. John was two years older than me, although in high school he'd only been one grade ahead of me. While we dated, he worked in sales at a furniture store called Right Time Rentals.

With John, I felt like I belonged. I felt like he cared for me—and in his own way, he did. For most of our relationship, John was nice. He didn't have a mean streak or temper. When we went out or spent time together, he'd show me how thoughtful he could be. A few times during my first year at WWU, he drove the two hours to see me and would bring me flowers. We only talked on the telephone a bit since this was before cell phones.

Ultimately, though, John's priority was himself and his friend group. He just enjoyed hanging out with his friends. They'd party, go golfing, and watch sports. He wasn't a jerk about it. He was a typical immature twenty-year-old guy.

One weekend, I came home from college, and we went to a party with mutual friends. For some reason, we left early. John drove me home and parked outside my house.

"Want to come in?" I asked.

"Nah, I'll see you tomorrow, though," he replied. I thought that was strange since it was only ten o'clock.

In my gut, I knew he went back to the party. I drove myself back and found him there. Upset, I confronted John. "Um, hi there! What are you doing back here?"

He never admitted to anything. We left the party—for the second time—together. I never figured out if he was there to see a girl behind my back or if he wanted to hang out with his guy friends without me. I avoided having a difficult conversation with him that would have revealed the truth.

For our second Christmas together, John gave me a tiny opal ring. We weren't anywhere special, like out to dinner. We were just standing outside next to each other when he handed me a blue velvet box with the ring in it.

Oh my gosh, I thought. *This is so sweet! He got me a ring!*

I leaned in and kissed John on the cheek. "Oh, it's beautiful. Thanks so much."

"Yeah," John said. "Mike picked it out."

I blinked.

Mike was John's boss at the furniture store. He was in his mid-to-late thirties and married with three stepdaughters. John may have thought Mike would know better what type of gift to give a woman. But even if that were true, he didn't say that or explain he was trying to do good and meant well by it.

Wow, I thought. *Way to ruin the moment.*

Telling me Mike picked out the ring was totally deflating. The ring didn't seem to mean anything to John beyond that it was a gift. He didn't even realize he'd taken all the joy out of the ring for me.

I wore it on my left finger like a promise ring, but I never forgot that John hadn't said anything to suggest it held a deeper meaning about our relationship.

Eventually, I realized our relationship wasn't going anywhere. My horizons were expanding; I was growing. On top of going to college, I'd gotten paid work as a filing clerk at a plastic surgeon's office and volunteer work in a pathology lab. Life had become busy for me, so John and I saw each other less and less.

From what I could tell, John wasn't moving forward. He hung out with the same friends, didn't seem to have any professional or career interests, and didn't try to prioritize our relationship. I couldn't see a future for us together.

John took it hard when I broke up with him. He sent me flowers and left a letter on the windshield of my car while I was at work, telling me he wanted to get back together.

I called John for the last time and told him, "No, I'm sorry. It's over."

Little did I know the next guy I'd date would show me what it really meant to lose my naïveté and innocence.

Dating Richard and Feeling Very Confused

Pretty much right after John and I broke up, I began dating a man named Richard. He was a few years older than me, and we were together for about three years. We met through Richard's mom Kara. I worked with her at the plastic surgeon's office. She was the head nurse and very kind and loving.

Richard had just moved back to Washington state from California and had recently broken up with his long-time girlfriend. One day he came into the office to visit Kara. I was smitten at first sight.

After he left, I scribbled my telephone number on a scrap of paper and held it out to Kara. "Would it be totally weird if I ask you to give your son my number?"

Kara laughed. "Not at all, hon."

Richard called me, and we started dating. He was good-looking, outgoing, and funny. He was also sweet at times and great with his young nieces, who were five and two years old.

Because I was so busy with school, work, and volunteering, we mostly saw each other on weekends. We went to some parties and hung out with some of his friends. Even trying hard, though, I didn't get a chance to see him every weekend. As a result, it took me a while to see his flaws.

One evening a friend and I went out for dinner at a restaurant that Richard often hung out at. He was there—and very out of it.

"I don't want you to see me like this," he slurred, extremely drunk.

It seemed so out of character, and I was incredibly confused. Slowly, I saw him get drunk more and more and realized this wasn't out of character at all.

Several months later, Richard bought me a beautiful bouquet of pink roses out of the blue. He shrugged, looking embarrassed. "I went to a party last night, and a girl from high school saw me. She told me she'd always had a crush on me." That only confused me more, and he didn't really explain himself further. Some part of me knew what he was saying, without coming right out and saying it. But I just sat there holding those flowers in my arms. I didn't—couldn't—get angry. I accepted it and didn't want to know anything more. I stuck my head in the sand, shoving that knowledge away, and we kept dating.

Throughout our relationship, Richard often didn't show up for me. When my grandfather died, I called him to see if he could pick me and my sister up from the airport after attending his funeral out of state because my mom and stepfather were staying longer.

"Sorry," he said, "I'm going out."

He left me a present on my doorstep to make up for it. I forgave him.

One afternoon I found drugs in his bedroom. "Richard, what's this? Why do you have this?"

He got mad and shoved me against the door. I called his mom, and she came over and confronted him. Once I found out he was not only drinking too much but also using drugs, his behavior made sense. By then, I was close to finishing nursing school, and I'd finally had enough. I broke up with him.

Months later Richard called and said he was sorry. He confessed that, yes, he'd been doing drugs and had cheated on me more than once. Richard was a child of divorce, and his own dad was a hard-nosed cop and not empathetic at all. This may have led him to develop the disease of addiction.

The evening when my friend and I had seen him at the restaurant, Richard hadn't been drunk. He'd been high on drugs. The time he bought me flowers out of the blue, Richard hadn't been doing something nice. He'd felt guilty. Those flowers had been his way of admitting and apologizing, without saying it explicitly, that he had slept with that girl at the party.

Why the heck is he telling me all this now? I wondered, hurt and baffled, as we spoke on the phone.

Dating Richard at that time in my life was ironic because I was working as a nursing aide at a center called Pediatric Interim Care. I had always loved babies and grew up babysitting. The care facility was in a converted house, and it took in drug-affected infants. They would arrive from the hospital to rehab the drugs in their system that their mothers had taken while pregnant. Some babies came to the center premature, some had compromised lungs, and others arrived in full drug withdrawal. It was heartbreaking, but Pediatric Interim Care made a big difference. It was amazing to see the babies recover. I always prayed they'd grow up healthy in the years to come. Long-term effects of in utero drug exposure include memory and learning disabilities, as well as behavior, language, and cognition problems.

The memory of one premature baby named Marcus will always stay with me. He came to the center with severe withdrawal. We had to keep him in a dark room to limit stimulation. He cried constantly, and the sounds of his cries affected all of us. He was at the center for months, but he was finally able to go to a foster home with his little body filled out and chubby from formula and love. I still have a photo of me holding him before he left for a foster home. The other nurses and I cried as we said goodbye because he had come so far, and we would miss him so much.

Richard never visited me at Pediatric Interim Care, although I talked about how rewarding the work was and invited him to stop by. Volunteers could sign up to rock the babies, but Richard wouldn't. After the truth came out about his addiction, I understood. Maybe Richard's guilt over his own drug use prevented him from looking at what addiction could do to babies. I'd spend much of my life trying to live healthily while the men in my life refused—or were unable—to do so.

I don't know why Richard contacted me and told me the truth, but I suspect he may have been doing a twelve-step program like Narcotics Anonymous. Contacting those you have harmed while using drugs is part of the program. I went to the student health center right after he called and got tested for sexually transmitted infections and HIV. As a nursing student, I knew his risky behavior put me in a dangerous position. I was a wreck waiting for the results. I felt angry and sad dealing with his confession. I was also mad at him and at myself for not following my intuition that was telling me something wasn't right. I had no idea what kinds of drugs he had used or who he had slept with. Luckily, the tests revealed I was healthy physically.

Looking back at that time, I had frequent stomachaches and was diagnosed with irritable bowel syndrome. I feel this was, in part, because I knew on a gut level (total pun intended) that he was not honest or faithful to me. I looked the other way, but my body was telling me the truth.

My experience dating Richard rattled my trust in men. It was also only the start of my codependent behavior. Countless times in my life, I've frozen when a romantic partner's bad behavior has been on display right in front of me. I spent years unable to deal with it, acting like if I didn't "see" or acknowledge it, then maybe it would go away. If I ignored it hard enough, then maybe I could convince myself it didn't really exist, and therefore, I wouldn't have to talk about it, confront my partner, and create conflict between us. If I didn't do any of that, then I could also convince myself that nothing had to change.

I learned that approach to bad behavior from growing up in a household with an alcoholic dad and a mom who refused to acknowledge it. The lack of acknowledgment that something was wrong within our family made me doubt my own intuition. For decades, this affected my ability to deal with conflict and to make sure my own needs were met. I didn't have a voice in any of my relationships with men who struggled with addiction—not as a child in my relationship with my dad, not in my romantic relationship with Richard, and not in my marriage to my husband Chad.

CHAPTER 6

My Marriage to Chad

I convinced myself everything would be okay

Marrying the Life of the Party

Chad and I were married for twenty-two years. We met when I was almost twenty-four years old, the same year I moved from Washington state to Arizona and began working as an RN. The day I met Chad, I'd just found out I passed my nursing boards, so I was loving life. My aunt Pam, who I was living with at the time, took me out to a bar and restaurant that the husband of one of Pam's friends owned. We had a great time.

As we drank, ate, and chatted with the people around us, Pam elbowed me and said, "Hey, you've got to meet this guy. He's from Seattle too."

I turned and there was Chad.

At the time, Chad's office was within walking distance to the bar, so he had gone there for dinner and drinks with one of his business partners. We talked and hit it off right away, chatting about how we'd both come from the Seattle area. Chad had attended a university in the Northwest. He was living in an apartment and was going through a divorce. He and his first wife had been married for only a couple of years, didn't have any kids, and had separated about six months ago.

Chad and I met in October 1993 and married a little over a year later. I approached him about the topic of marriage. Chad said he didn't want to lose me, and, yes, we should get married. Not exactly the most mature way to decide to get married on both our parts. We set the wedding for two months later in Washington state. It made sense at the time considering most of our family lived in Washington. We could celebrate Christmas with them and have the wedding right after. Soon after we married, Chad and I bought a house near Phoenix. Our first son Westin was born three years later in 1997. We waited four years before having our second son Wyatt, who was born in early 2001.

I know now that we didn't date long enough before getting married. We should have taken more time to get to know each other away from all the parties, laughs, and fun, and really consider the lifestyles we each wanted to live over the long term. I was still so young and naïve. Looking back, I'm sure he needed more time after his divorce, and I needed more time to mature and know myself after graduating from college. That isn't what society taught me though. Most of my friends were already married, and some were having babies. I felt like I was behind in life. This urgency mindset did me a disservice to my own growth as a person.

The first time I went to Chad's apartment, I saw a framed photo of a woman in his guest room/office. I assumed it was his sister but later learned he had been dating a woman when we first met. He broke up with her to date me. We never spoke about this, and I didn't ask who the woman was when I saw the picture.

I found out about her after we got married from one of his friends. A few weeks before our wedding, we went to Chad's company Christmas party. It was the first time I really noticed that Chad tended to over-drink. He left the party with another guy, disappearing for a while. It felt like they were up to no good, but I did not confront him. It upset me, and something felt wrong, but afterward I convinced myself everything would be okay once we got married.

Chad had a real entrepreneurial spirit. At the beginning of our relationship, Chad owned an apartment property management business with two partners, a pair of stepbrothers. They bought Chad out of that business, and he used the capital to start his own property management company about a year into our marriage. Over time, his property management work evolved into real estate investment. He started by buying existing apartment buildings in the Phoenix metropolitan area.

In 2001, Chad brought on a partner, Ray. From there, the business grew into a portfolio that also included properties in different states. Building that type of company success meant Chad had to socialize often outside regular working hours, wining and dining clients, investors, and colleagues at restaurants and bars. For us as a couple, this meant spending much more time out of the house with other people than at home enjoying each other's company. Much, much later, for Chad it also meant buying flashy cars, playing many rounds of golf, and globe-trotting. Through years of hard work, Chad's original business grew into multiple companies, and the many hats he wore came to include real estate advisor to a well-known American businessman who is also the author of a popular series of books about personal finances and financial literacy. As part of his advisor role, Chad traveled the world, and sometimes I'd go with him. I went on several great trips to some amazing places.

Chad was the life of the party. Unfortunately, not all of life is a party.

When I was eight months pregnant with Westin, I met Chad and his friend Paul for dinner. After we finished eating, I went home to get some much-needed sleep while Chad and Paul stayed out. Around midnight, the sound of the front door opening and closing woke me up, which I thought was odd. Chad usually came in through the garage. I left the bedroom to find Chad and Paul had both come inside.

They were acting strangely, and I asked, "What happened?"

"We hit a tree at the end of the street," Chad replied.

A police officer came to the door and asked for them. When she saw how pregnant I was, she didn't give Chad, who'd been driving, a breathalyzer test. I don't think she would have been legally allowed to conduct a breathalyzer test since he'd left the scene, and she hadn't witnessed the collision. He wasn't arrested or given a citation.

This is what happened: Chad and Paul were almost home, and Chad took a right-hand turn onto our street too fast and crashed into a palm tree. He was driving a brand-new two-seater BMW that he'd owned for all of two weeks. I wasn't thrilled with his choices that night, especially since we were about to have a baby. Chad didn't learn anything from the incident. His car was totaled, yet he ended up getting paid more for it from the insurance than what he'd originally paid.

After Westin was born, things got worse. Our relationship definitely began to shift once we had children. For me, it was time to grow up, stay home more, and build a family together. That put a damper on the life Chad wanted to live. He didn't want to stop partying, whether he was with friends or clients. When he went out at night, Chad would call me on the landline (this was long before cell phones) and tell me he would be home in an hour. Two or three hours would pass, and he'd call again and say he'd be home soon. It felt lonely and frustrating. I had a hard time sleeping until I knew he was home. It scared me that he was probably drinking and driving. It triggered me back to my childhood, when I couldn't fall asleep until I heard my dad come in the front door after being out at the bar. When Chad did get home, he often reeked of alcohol, which was *not* a turn-on for me. I asked him numerous times to take a cab home if he had been drinking, but he never did.

Over many years I discovered that Chad coped with life by using humor, alcohol, or toxic positivity. I don't intend to shame him by saying this. He learned to use these things to cope with growing up in his dysfunctional family. But it was difficult to have a deep, connected relationship with someone who dismissed my feelings. He was not okay with me being sad or angry. He considered tears manipulative and would even say that to our kids. We parented very differently and did not agree on how boys should be brought up. Like many men of his era, he was raised with the "men don't cry" attitude and worse: "Don't be a pussy." I disagreed with this archaic and abusive philosophy because it puts men down who aren't supposedly behaving "masculine" enough. I didn't want my boys adopting these harmful views of themselves as men. There were just too many differences in parenting styles between me and Chad for us to have a healthy relationship.

I became resentful of Chad's drinking, and he probably became resentful of me too. We both started moving further and further from each other, and we could never figure out how to get back to what we'd had at the beginning of our relationship. Neither one of us had the tools to work through these huge differences. That made for a long two decades.

A Toxic Relationship

When Westin was two years old, we went to California to visit some friends: Lisa, Tony, and others. One night, Lisa's parents watched Westin while we went out. We had a fun time at dinner, followed by more fun dancing. Lisa and I spent most of the night out on the dance floor, singing along to the live band. Chad and Tony hung out most of the night, flirting with our other friend's attractive wife. At one point, Tony was wearing her bra over his shirt, and Chad was wearing her jacket. I wasn't sure how that had happened. I drank more than I normally did, and by the time we got home, I was exhausted. I headed up to the bedroom we were sharing with our two-year-old, who was fast asleep. Barely able to keep my eyes open, I wanted to go right to sleep. Chad wanted to get intimate.

I batted him away, tired. The next thing I knew, Chad's hands were around my neck, strangling me. I could not fight him off.

"You were teasing me all night long," he said repeatedly.

I wasn't even with you all night! I thought, panicking. *Is this how I'm going to die?*

I remember praying to God for Chad to let go of my neck. He did.

The next day, my neck was bruised and hurt badly. Every time I swallowed I could feel it. I told Lisa what had happened. She didn't say anything. I confronted Chad, and he had no reply. It felt like no one was hearing me or cared at all. Chad acted like he was learning about it for the first time, like he had no memory of what he'd done. He'd been physically abusive while blackout drunk.

I stuffed my trauma down and ignored it—for years.

Over time it came to feel like Chad and I weren't in a loving relationship at all. He was always gone, working or socializing, which most often meant having drinks. While I did go on a few trips with him when he was traveling, more often than not, I chose to stay home with our sons. Chad and I did not have a strong emotional connection to begin with, and this drastic difference in lifestyles only made it worse. I needed nurturing, caring, communication, and time from him. He didn't give me any of that.

One day I asked Chad, "Could you be home tonight to have dinner with us?"

"I'm an entrepreneur," he said. "I don't work nine to five." And that was that.

When I was seven months pregnant with our second child Wyatt, I suffered from terrible insomnia. Chasing after Westin, an active three-year-old, was really hard every day. One particularly rough week, I only had two or three hours of sleep each night. I was so emotionally and physically exhausted that I started crying and decided to call Chad at the office. I rarely called him at work. The call went through to his secretary Sabrina. So much stress and strain had built up inside me that I couldn't stop crying to talk clearly.

"Okay, let me see if I can get Chad on the phone for you," Sabrina said quickly.

Chad finally came on the line. "Can you come home?" I asked, still crying. "I need help. Please, just come home. I'm exhausted, and I need a break."

Chad didn't come home. Instead, he yelled at me. "Don't you ever do this again!"

I was absolutely shocked. Instead of compassion, I was met with harsh dismissal. This couldn't be the man I married. I realized then that Chad was not going to help me. I was on my own. I'd have to figure out how to parent two boys and take care of myself alone. I couldn't rely on my husband to be an equal co-parent or to care about my emotional needs. The only guess I have for why he acted the way he did was that Sabrina may have freaked out and alarmed Chad when she passed the call to him, so he thought something disastrous had happened. When he realized no one was having a physical emergency, he became upset—not the reaction I was looking for or needed. I felt completely ignored emotionally.

Eventually, he asked, "Are you okay now?"

Stuffing down my shock, I said, "Yep."

We hung up. Neither one of us ever brought up what happened or talked about it. I'm sure he was clueless, and I was disappointed and sad. I ignored this for years until I started deep diving into therapy and realized how unsafe I felt in my marriage.

One summer, Chad had a group of business acquaintances in town for a golf tournament. After they finished playing eighteen holes, I joined them for dinner and drinks. We hung out on the golf club's patio. I'd never met most of the men before, but a woman named Erin came over who had participated in the fitness boot camp that I ran when I was a personal trainer, so I didn't feel entirely out of place—that is, until Chad spoke up.

I don't remember how the topic of conversation came up, but Chad suddenly said, "Yeah, married sex sucks." He announced this loudly in front of Erin and all these other men. It didn't seem like he'd had much to drink, but he sure didn't have a filter.

One of the men who'd come in for the tournament, who I didn't know, called Chad out. "Hey man, wait a minute. That's inappropriate to say, period, but especially in front of your wife."

Chad laughed and half-heartedly tried to backtrack. "Well, you know," he joked, "you guys probably all agree."

I was incredibly embarrassed, but I didn't say anything. I didn't have any voice.

When my second son Wyatt was six weeks old, Chad and I were invited to a charity dinner. I was breastfeeding and hadn't lost all the baby weight from my pregnancy, so none of my clothes fit. My mom was visiting, and we went to a consignment shop to find a dress for me to wear. I was always a conservative spender.

On the night of the dinner, Mom babysat Wyatt and Westin, who was three years old. I felt comfortable and excited for a night out, even if I had to bring my breast pump and use it on the car ride home. The evening went well. We had a great night dining, dancing, and socializing with friends at our table.

We left the event around eleven thirty at night and headed home. I was tired but happy as I pumped. Exiting the freeway, Chad asked, "Left or right?"

Right would take us home, so I said, "Right."

Chad replied cheerfully, "Nope." He turned left, then drove us to a bar nearby.

I was so caught off guard that I didn't say anything. We went into the bar, and I ordered a water. Chad wanted to dance, so we danced. I felt completely dismissed. I was dead on my feet and concerned about getting home to my newborn, relieving my mom, and sneaking in some sleep before the baby woke up again.

Have you ever tried dancing while mad at your partner? It's not fun. I was less than thrilled to be there.

Chad stopped us and said, "If you don't start acting like you want to be here, I'll find someone who will."

My stomach dropped. I felt scared and hurt. I believed Chad when he said if he didn't get what he wanted, he would cheat on me, divorce me, and not love me anymore. I had two little boys to think of, and he was threatening the life we had built together. I felt like I was being held hostage. The sense of being so alone and powerless was horrible. The lack of acknowledgement, the dismissal of my feelings, and the threats created a deep sense of danger in me, which continued to unravel the trust and connection we had when we got married.

Today I would never tolerate someone threatening me like this. Thankfully now there is Lyft and Uber to contact quickly if you need to get out of an unsafe situation, but at that time in my life and marriage, I didn't know how to stand up for myself. This is one of several related reasons why I quit drinking at forty-two.

In my early forties, I began to evaluate alcohol in my life. When I was in high school, I threw up once from drinking too much, but never again. Funny how some lessons we learn quickly and others it takes decades. I had too much to drink on occasion in my younger days, but mostly I was a light drinker. As I got into my forties, one or two glasses of wine, which is what I drank, did not make me feel well. I realize now that I was perimenopausal, which was causing me to sleep terribly. If I drank even a small amount of alcohol, my sleep would get even worse. Along with my desire to live a healthy lifestyle, I began to see that alcohol wasn't serving me and I could live without it. I also began to be completely turned off by the party atmosphere and drinking.

I realized that I had to keep myself safe. I didn't feel safe with Chad, physically, mentally, or emotionally. On so many occasions, I couldn't tell if he legitimately was unable to remember something he'd said or done to me—like when he choked me—or if he was lying about it and trying to gaslight me. If I had been drinking, I'd doubt myself more or just forget about it, stuffing down all the emotions, so I stopped drinking. Because Chad drank whenever we went out, I was already the designated driver. I never wanted to jeopardize my physical safety, and I couldn't rely on him to drive sober.

On top of all that, when I drank, I lost my voice. It made me even less capable of standing up for myself. On those few occasions when I tried to speak up and deal with something difficult in our relationship, Chad would shut me down. More than once, he said bluntly, "That happened yesterday. Move on!"

Chad treated my attempts to speak with him as ruining all his fun. He'd shut me down by calling me a buzzkill or Debbie Downer. To him, that type of open communication about tough topics wasn't useful or necessary; instead, it was just dwelling on the negative.

I was also a buzzkill in other ways. On a trip we took to New Orleans, Chad and I went out, spent time together, and enjoyed ourselves. We went to an NBA game, then went to dinner and out to a few bars. As the night went on, it got late, and I got tired.

"Okay," I told Chad. "I'm done. Let's go home."

"What? No, I don't want to go home," he replied. "Don't be a buzzkill." That's how Chad dealt with me—controlled me—whenever he was at risk of potentially not getting what he wanted.

When the boys were young, we got season tickets to the Arizona Cardinals. We all loved football. For one of Westin's birthdays, Chad and I had a message shown on the stadium's jumbotron: *Happy Birthday, Westin! Love, Mom, Dad, and Wyatt.*

Westin loved it. It went off without a hitch, and we got a great photo of it.

Two weeks later, we went to another football game—this time on *my* birthday. There, up on the jumbotron, completely unexpectedly, I saw: *Happy birthday, Mom! Love, Westin and Wyatt.*

Chad's name wasn't mentioned in the birthday message, even though he paid for it. It was also written to *Mom*, not to *Laura*, which made it seem like he didn't see me as his wife, the person with whom he was married, or even as a person who has feelings and deserves love, respect, and consideration. The only meaning or value I seemed to have to him was as his sons' mom. I was already feeling unseen, unheard, and like I didn't matter to Chad. This birthday message seemed to be more proof of that and only made me feel worse.

After the game, I joked to Chad, "Oh, my name is Mom? Not Laura? That sign wasn't from you? It was just from the boys?"

"God, you're so ungrateful about everything," he said.

I shut up after that, unwilling to find out if I'd misinterpreted the jumbotron message and unwilling to explain anymore how I really felt. How could I when he told me I was ungrateful? It stung. At that time in our lives, I was taking care of the entire household—like my mom had done when I was a kid—while working part-time and volunteering at the kids' school and at our church. Chad was gone often, working late or traveling for work. Part of me accepted what I was being told: *Don't voice your needs or wants. Just be grateful for how things are, even if you disagree and it makes you feel bad.*

My needs, wants, and voice held little to no weight for Chad, and I didn't know how to ask him to be a real partner. Because I grew up in a household where my dad wasn't a real partner to my mom, I was conditioned to accept a marriage like this. Because I grew up going to church and learning that good girls must subordinate their needs and wants to everyone else's—to take care of everyone else, to never express anger—I was conditioned to keep silent and let Chad dictate how our relationship would work. When I did speak up, he'd dismiss or disapprove of my concerns. At the time, I didn't have the knowledge, skills, or standards to get my needs met.

I wasn't the only person in our marriage whose childhood shaped what we grew up to expect from our relationships or how we behaved in them. Chad's dad was an alcoholic too. When he was a child, his dad would get drunk, aggressive, and abusive. Sometimes when it got especially threatening, his mom would take the kids out of the house. While this was probably the safest option she had at the time, it also modeled for Chad that whenever conflict arises, it's best to remove yourself from the situation or avoid it.

Whenever I tried to open a dialogue about our relationship, Chad perceived it as conflict, so he would avoid, deflect, or suppress it. As a natural workaholic whose professional success was tied to his self-worth, Chad's business gave him an easy out; to remove himself from our home, all he had to do was go to work. At the office, where he was the boss, Chad was surrounded by people who always said yes to him. What conflict there was, he could control.

In this chapter, I've described a variety of moments from my marriage to Chad. They are not meant to be a list of gripes and grievances. They weren't an everyday occurrence; remember, Chad and I were married for more than two decades. They are not meant to portray Chad as a villain or mastermind intent on victimizing me.

These moments are meant to show how, without open and honest communication, without reflection about your compatibility with your partner, without self-assurance and confidence in yourself as an individual, and without a commitment by both partners to nurture your trust and love for each other, relationships can turn toxic. How many of us wake up one day to find we don't recognize ourselves or our partners anymore? How many of us wonder how everything could have gone so wrong? I have no doubt that married women everywhere can point to similar versions of these moments that they've lived through in their own relationships.

When we experience these moments, we need to know how to react intentionally and assertively in ways that help us learn, grow, and protect ourselves. Otherwise, we're letting ourselves be trapped in lives we don't deserve and don't have to settle for. In the next chapter, I show how these types of moments continued to build up in my marriage—until I'd finally had enough and stopped settling for a life I didn't want.

CHAPTER 7

The High Cost of Golden Cuffs

I paid a huge price

Chad's Alcoholism

Ten years into our marriage, Chad got a DWI. In fact, Chad and my father got DWIs the same year—Dad in January 2005 and Chad in November 2005. Dad's experience caused him to get sober. Chad's experience didn't lead to sobriety.

Chad actually got his first DWI at the age of twenty-two, before we knew each other. That early experience helped Chad gain some awareness of his father's alcoholism. It helped him look at some of his family dynamics, and soon after, his family held an intervention for his father Bob. They told their father he had to get sober, or he would lose his family. Bob got sober after that, but I don't think anyone in the family sought any counseling. Unfortunately, Chad's second DWI in 2005 didn't change his perspective about his drinking or the role his father's abuse and alcoholism might have played in his own drinking problem starting when he was a young man.

At the time, Chad and I were seeing a counselor, Betsy. I was seeing her myself, and Chad and I were seeing her together. At an appointment with her by myself, I told Betsy about Chad's DWI.

"Well, I can't talk about it with Chad unless he brings it up himself," she said.

"What?" I couldn't believe it. I accepted Betsy's position, though, because I thought she must know best. After many more years of therapy, I came to understand she'd done us a huge disservice. I was looking for help with how to address the root causes of Chad's behavior and how worried I was about him drinking and driving, and I didn't get that help from her. I knew his childhood trauma was causing his alcohol abuse and affecting our life and marriage. I wanted him to get help.

Chad's DWI could have been a turning point. If it had been addressed in counseling, it might have helped him, me, and our marriage. It was frustrating and, on top of Betsy's silence and his abusive behavior, I felt a new level of helplessness and isolation. Chad wasn't shown much compassion in his childhood, so he didn't develop any compassion. He was rarely able to feel for another person or consider how his behavior affected them. Empathy was foreign to him. That's also part of the disease of addiction. How he acted is not excusable, but these are all recognized markers.

I'd lived through years of sleepless nights, scared to death that Chad was going to get himself or someone else killed while driving drunk. Then, when he finally got a DWI, part of me thought, *Oh thank you, God. No one was injured, and this can be a wake-up call.*

It wasn't, though. Chad had to attend some meetings and spend his nights in Tent City, the makeshift, outdoor jail that former Maricopa County Sheriff Joe Arpaio opened in 1993 to deal with overcrowding. Chad could still go to work during the day, and he didn't tell many people he was there. We told the kids he was traveling. He also lost his driver's license for a while. He solved that problem by hiring a car service. None of these consequences appeared to change Chad's drinking.

One night, many years later, we went to a bar with a rowdy group of friends. I hit the outdoor dance floor with Susan, a woman I knew well. For a while, we were having a great time. The music was fantastic, the crowd was just the right size, and everyone was in a fun—not sloppy—mood. I liked dancing, and I was enjoying myself.

From across the dance floor, I saw Chad lounging on an outdoor couch on the patio. A young woman was sitting on his lap. I left Susan and went out to my husband. I didn't want to make a scene, so I circled around to the woman's back, tapped her on the shoulder, and smiled as I told her to get up and get off his lap. I had to tell her twice before she got up and left. I didn't say anything to Chad.

A few days later I brought up what had happened. Chad gave me a confused, impatient look. "I thought she was a waitress and we'd get better service."

I was dumbfounded. He was trying to justify and explain away what he'd done, and so badly too. I didn't think he even remembered the woman on his lap and pulled that excuse out of thin air.

Why would you ever have anyone else in your lap, whether they're a waitress or not?

"I don't want to be around you anymore if you've been drinking," I said, taking a stand for once. "If you're with me, I want you to be sober, okay? This is important to me."

"Okay," he agreed dismissively.

In retrospect, I really wanted Chad to quit drinking and get help. His binge drinking was harmful to me and himself. I did not have the confidence to say this to him, as I feared he would say no, and I would have to make some hard decisions that I wasn't prepared to make yet.

It made me wonder what Chad was doing when I wasn't there. But because he so often dismissed what I said about his behavior—like having some random woman on his lap—and wasn't willing to take accountability, I'd drop it. I never pushed anything with him beyond what he would allow. I do think Chad wanted us to have a better marriage. Ultimately, though, he didn't want to look at his drinking and partying habits or his workaholism.

Soon after that conversation about the woman sitting on Chad's lap, we went to a friend's fiftieth birthday party. I was sober and expected Chad to be too because I'd asked him not to drink around me. But as I rounded a corner, I saw him knock back a shot. I don't think he saw me standing there, and I never said anything to him about it.

You're going to do whatever you want, I thought with such clarity at that moment, *just like you always have.*

That was one of a couple key turning points that I now recognize were the beginning of the end. I lost trust and respect for my husband. After that, I knew Chad was sneaking alcohol, and nothing I could say would matter. Even after I'd asked him not to, Chad couldn't *not* drink, or he didn't want to *not* drink. I realized I had repeated the same pattern of marrying an alcoholic that my mother had modeled for me. I've asked myself so many times how I ended up in a decades-long relationship with a man who had the same type of problem with alcohol as my dad did. I now know the answer to my own question: I was trying to subconsciously fix my dad's alcoholism. Since I was comfortable in that role, I repeated it by trying to fix Chad's alcoholism too.

Another key turning point, or maybe the straw that broke the camel's back, took place just before the 2015 Thanksgiving holiday. Chad's mom Claire lives in Washington state. She came down to visit us in Arizona for Thanksgiving. Before she arrived, I came down with a virus that wasn't going away.

"You're still sick?" Chad said at one point, annoyed.

Claire flew in on a Friday, and that night we talked about our weekend plans.

"Oh yeah, tomorrow I'm taking the boys and going four-wheeling with some of the guys," Chad said.

I was surprised and taken aback. He hadn't mentioned that plan before.

You're what? I thought, so perplexed. *Seriously?*

Chad's mom had just gotten into town, and he only saw her once or twice a year. And now he was going off without any consideration for her.

The next morning, Chad and the boys left. I was still not feeling well at all. If anything, I felt worse. Soon after, I turned to Claire.

"Claire, I have to take myself to the hospital," I told her. "I just feel terrible."

At the hospital, I found out that I had pericardial effusion, a buildup of excess fluid in the pericardial cavity around my heart. Symptoms include chest pain, shortness of breath, fatigue, swelling, and low blood pressure—and it can impair the heart's ability to function effectively. It can be caused by an infection, pericarditis, kidney failure, trauma, and more. While I only had extreme fatigue, it was enough for me to know something was not right with me.

It was a serious health issue.

"We're going to have to keep you overnight and do more test-ing to see if we have to perform a pericardiocentesis, where we go in and drain the fluid," a doctor informed me.

I called the house several times, but Claire didn't pick up. She would never presume to answer someone else's phone. I called Chad; he didn't answer either.

I got ahold of my side of the family, and they promptly all came up to the hospital. My sister, dad, mom, and stepfather were all there to support me and find out what was going on.

Fortunately, the tests determined that the doctors didn't have to drain the fluid, and the issue would resolve on its own.

Chad finally showed up that evening. Even though he brought flowers, I was tired and upset.

This was a defining moment toward the end of our marriage. Chad's inconsiderate, self-centered ways were on full display. First, he disrespected his mother by going off on a guys' outing instead of spending time with her. On top of that, he didn't care that I'd been sick or ended up in the hospital. That was an incon-venience, and he thought I was playing it up for attention. Let me tell you, I have never been that person. Being laid up drives me bonkers.

When we got home from the hospital, I was all out of restraint. "Don't you ever do that again," I told him. "Your mother came here to spend time with you, her grandsons, and us as a family."

I was particularly protective of Claire because of what she had suffered in her own marriage to an alcoholic and abuser. She would never in a million years complain or say anything to Chad about his behavior. This made me see in a new light that Chad was treating me the same way he treated his mom, and that some aspects of how he treated us were similar to how Chad's dad had treated Claire. As an adult, Chad had grown up to mirror what had been modeled for him.

Chad was also treating the two of us, who were supposed to be the most important women in his life, like we were both stuck in the same "good girl" trap. He expected us to accommodate whatever he wanted to do, suppress our emotions, and not complain. I'm not sure Claire could see the "good girl" trap she was in, but I could—and I wanted out.

Chad and I separated the following year, during the summer of 2016. Westin had just graduated from high school, and we told our boys what was happening. Chad went up to Idaho that June, where we had a summer house, and Westin decided to go with him. Wyatt had to take a summer class, so I took responsibility for getting him to and from school in South Scottsdale. He finished right before the Fourth of July, so I sent Wyatt to join his father and brother. Over the years, we'd spent several summers in Idaho and had friends up there.

Two days later, Chad called me. The boys had invited friends over and had gotten ahold of some alcohol. One of the other boys ended up very sick. Then another boy freaked out and called 911. When I asked where *he* was during this incident, Chad told me he was upstairs.

Trying to remain calm, I thought, *Who's the adult here? What were you doing? Were you drunk? Were these kids really unsupervised?*

The incident seemed bizarre. It was the first time I felt like I was by myself, "off duty," while my boys were with their dad. Chad was the parent in charge, and someone could have been seriously harmed. He was responsible for dealing with the ambulance, police, and boys' parents—not me. Everything ended up okay, but for me, it showed how things were starting to change in our family and relationship dynamics.

In families experiencing alcoholism, avoiding the issues is common. Families may enable the addiction to continue by shielding the addict from the negative consequences of their actions.

This behavior is called codependence. I was codependent. I've worked hard to recover from codependency. I attended Al-Anon for about eight months. This is a program for families and people affected by another person's alcoholism. Al-Anon helped me take the focus off the alcoholics in my life and look at myself and my own behavior, both for how I was avoiding various issues and how I wanted to live my life. It also helped me see I had a choice about how I wanted to live. I was not stuck in this kind of life. I chose to stay for years. Then I chose to leave and take care of myself. I was not responsible for fixing anyone but myself.

My Finances and Body Image Struggles

I'm incredibly grateful that my marriage to Chad gave us two amazing sons. I did find it mentally difficult when I stopped working as an RN to be a stay-at-home mom. Relying on someone else's finances felt risky and a vulnerable position to be in. At times, it also felt demoralizing, especially because no matter what people may say, I don't think society respects women who stay home with their kids—by far the hardest job I've ever had.

Once, for example, Chad and I were signing the paperwork for a new property we were buying. Chad would sign on a line, then I'd sign beside him. In one section of the paperwork, only Chad, the primary signer, was needed. I asked Margaret, the title representative facilitating the sale, if I needed to sign there too.

"No, not there," she said.

"Oh, why not?"

"Well, if you went and got a job, you could sign there."

It felt like someone had slapped me in the face. She could have just said, "No, you don't need to sign there." She didn't even know me. It was demeaning and disrespectful for her to say that and in the way she said it. She assumed I didn't have a job. I *did* have a job as a full-time stay-at-home mom. I was also teaching spin classes at the time while studying to become a certified personal trainer. On top of that, I was a registered nurse. But there I was in that office, exercising a financial responsibility that would have real legal and financial consequences if anything went wrong, yet she didn't respect me as a full partner with my husband, especially since she didn't view me as a professional anything. I was "just" a wife and mother.

Why was I signing that paperwork alongside Chad? Early on in his business, I was a partner in the business, accepting all the responsibility and benefits that entails, including signing loan applications and other legal documents. Although I wasn't active in the day-to-day business, nor did I have the knowledge to run operations, I was still a partner. I was privy to a lot of information about the very successful business, but that didn't translate into personal success, respect from my husband, or financial security for me. That was tough.

The benefits of that comfortable life, were extremely shallow. They weren't what I wanted from a relationship. What I wanted from the beginning was a deep connection and a real partner who respected me. I didn't have that.

Subconsciously, I spent a long stretch of our marriage trying to get Chad's attention. I ate super healthy, cut out all sugar, and exercised regularly. My health was very important to me and a big motivator. Trying to look and feel more attractive so maybe my husband would give me some attention was the icing on the cake. It felt like I would never be thin enough or pretty enough to compete with his drinking, partying, and the other women around him. That didn't stop me from wanting Chad to choose me.

Chad was a direct person, which served him well in business. I was not a business, though. Nor was our marriage. Although Chad didn't control how much money I could use, I still

73

felt a power imbalance between us in more subtle ways. In the early years of the business, Jenna, one of the teenagers who babysat for us, began selling Cutco kitchen knives. She did a little sales presentation for me and asked if I wanted to buy any from her. The Cutco brand can get expensive, so I told her, "I have to check with my husband."

When I called Chad at work to make sure it was okay to purchase them, he said, "What? Those knives cost how much? No!"

I didn't buy the knives, and I lost a babysitter because Jenna felt let down and didn't want to have anything to do with us anymore.

Years later, after the business had grown by leaps and bounds, I bought a Vitamix blender. Even then, Chad questioned how much it cost. "You spent how much on a blender?"

All I could think was, *You're bitching at me about a blender when you have how many expensive cars?*

To this day, I still have that Vitamix, so I'm pretty sure it was a smart investment!

Both my parents grew up poor and successfully built better, middle-class lives for me and my sister. Not surprisingly, getting a good education, securing a stable job, and prioritizing financial security were hammered into me. While some of these were valuable, it also limited my lens for seeing what I could do with my life. To increase my financial literacy, I read books on real estate and real estate investing. By studying these books and attending live seminars, I learned to think outside the box of my upbringing and shift my perspective about what was possible for my career and my future.

Financial literacy helped me separate myself from parts of my upbringing that didn't serve me. It helped me move past certain fears in my life, gave me confidence to become an entrepreneur, and taught me how to invest in real estate. Eventually, I used what I learned to start my own health and wellness business and buy real estate. Financial independence and freedom are essential for women to build the lives they deserve.

One of the most difficult experiences related to the financial imbalance between me and my husband, which impacted my body image and autonomy. Having had a lifelong challenge with my looks and body, after breastfeeding both my babies, I became insecure about my breasts. Like many new mothers after their pregnancies, the image I had of my changed body suffered and was slow to recover. A woman's "ideal" body image is shoved in our faces from the time we are young. I really feel for the young women today who are dealing with all the filtered images on social media that look so real but never could be. It's impossible to live up to those norms and expectations. At this time in my life, I was definitely influenced by the media and feeling particularly negative about myself.

I decided to get breast implants, which was fairly common among my friends after they'd had children. Chad was all for me getting them and never complained about the cost. After I had them done, I told the doctor, "They're bigger than I hoped."

The doctor replied, "Well, that's the smallest implant."

Uncomfortable, all I could think to say was, "Okay."

I lived with them for about eight years. My health and wellness journey led me to become very athletic, even running a half-marathon for my fortieth birthday. The size of my breasts began to negatively affect me. They were too large for my frame and physically uncomfortable. They had never been what I intended anyway, so I decided to have the implants removed. I also thought about the health implications in the future that might affect me if I kept them.

When I told Chad my decision, he scoffed. "You're never going to be satisfied, are you?"

He wasn't supportive. He wasn't willing to help me improve my quality of life. He didn't want to listen to me.

"I'm not paying for that," Chad announced.

You're not telling me what to do with my body, I thought.

It took me a year of teaching Pilates classes to earn enough money to pay for the surgery. All the while, I saw the big purchases Chad made. He came home with a new Range Rover, Lamborghini, Ferrari, and even a vintage '57 Chevy, often without saying anything about them beforehand. It felt awful to not have his support emotionally or financially.

"It's an investment," he claimed.

To take care of paying our bills, I had access to a joint checking account I used. But if I needed money to be added to the account, I had to contact the accountant at Chad's office to transfer the funds. It didn't feel right having to ask an accountant to transfer money into my own account. Chad had to ask the accountant to transfer funds too, but he also had direct access to all the business accounts to get cash whenever he wanted. At the time, because I thought he "made all the money," he deserved to buy whatever he wanted. I was, however, often hurt that as his wife and supposed life partner, he didn't include me in his decision-making, especially about large purchases. For instance, one time he bought a cabin on a golf course in Idaho without consulting me. He said he thought it was a great deal and hyped it up so I'd be on board.

Thankfully, Chad didn't nickel and dime me over a new dress or groceries, but I had to psych myself up if I wanted to talk with him about my own large purchases, such as when I wanted to have my breast implants taken out or using some of our money for my business. That felt unfair and demeaning. In general, I didn't spend money on large purchases. I shopped at Nordstrom Rack and Target. When it came to money, I focused on paying attention to our monthly household expenses and anything we needed to buy for our kids.

While Chad and I were separated and in mediation, the mediation lawyer advised us not to make any large purchases, so I didn't. Meanwhile, in Idaho, Chad bought another car—and a boat. After our divorce, I've been able to spend money on whatever I want without consulting anyone. *That* has been very liberating.

Today I would never join my finances with someone else's, even if I found the best fantasy man in the world. Joining finances, especially for women, can become golden cuffs that come with a heavy price. Even though I lived in a nice house in a nice neighborhood and never wanted for anything materially, I was far from happy.

Although I feel lucky to be in the financial position that I'm in now, I also paid a huge price for what I have. Even after twenty-two years of marriage and taking care of our boys, when we split up, Chad claimed, "I did all the work, and you still get half." When he said that, I got that he didn't ever really respect me or the work I did as his wife and the mother of his children.

At one point, I learned he had invested four times the amount in his friend's company than he had told me. Dumbfounded, I asked myself why he wouldn't have told me this. I had trusted Chad to make many investments over the years and took him at this word. I didn't question how much he invested, and I assumed he would be honest. Learning this new information shook my trust that he'd be fair and honest with me in the divorce, so I hired a lawyer and a forensic CPA to look into the business and financials. I felt disappointed to have to do it but knew I needed to protect myself. While the CPA and lawyers made sure every-thing was fair, they dragged the divorce process on for nearly four years.

While working part-time and studying to educate myself for a new career, I coordinated everything for our kids, driving them to and from school and all their sports and activities. I made sure they got all their homework done. I loved getting to be with my kids, but I also felt overwhelmed having to do it by myself. We also had three dogs to care for. I wanted a partner to co-parent with me, whereas Chad just wanted me to hire household help for myself. To him, this was what I signed up for when we got married, and I should be grateful I had a nice life.

My nice life got incredibly lonely over the years. While I had plenty of friends, events, and activities to occupy my time, I missed the connection and attention I needed from a partner.

One Friday night I drove to a grocery store called AJ's and bought two desserts. Chad was out with his friends, and so were the boys. As they got older, I knew Wyatt and Westin were supposed to spend more time outside the home—a valuable thing. They were growing up. But it meant I spent more time alone.

I sat in that AJ's parking lot and ate both of those desserts alone in my car. It was the epitome of eating my emotions and very unlike me; I hardly ever ate sweets at that time in my life. I just felt so alone. Sitting there, it hit me in a way that hadn't happened before. I didn't have a partner. I didn't want this for the rest of my life. I deserved better.

In the end, I would have given anything for Chad to be a present partner—in marriage and in parenting. I wanted him to show up emotionally and physically, not only financially. He showed up for the kids when he was around, but he couldn't show up for me. He even had the audacity to claim he didn't feel supported when I chose not to travel with him. I tried to balance it all and please everyone, but I wanted to be a present parent—the type of parent I always wanted.

Hello, we have two children? I thought incredulously. *I can't drop everything when you spring an invitation on me at the last minute.*

Parenting requires planning every day. My mom and stepfather Harlan helped me on multiple occasions by taking care of the kids so I could go on trips with Chad, but they traveled also and couldn't always do that for us. Chad didn't have the capacity to put situations like this in perspective. It was all about what was best for him and what he wanted. He couldn't look at the bigger picture of what was best for me, our kids, and our family. You can't force someone to look at something differently without their willingness. We do what we know and how we grow up.

Once our boys were grown, I finally realized that I could choose how I wanted to live, and Chad could choose how he wanted to live. I had that power. I didn't want to live the way Chad did, and he didn't want to live the way I did. It seems like a simple thing. But in a long-term relationship, this can be hard to realize, acknowledge, and accept. It's not that I was living in denial, precisely. It was that I struggled with codependency and did not have the proper tools or maturity to identify the fundamental incompatibility in our relationship, and that it would never be possible to change our incompatibility. For so long, I thought I had to stay in a life that did not fulfill me or make me happy. I didn't.

Chad is not the devil or a villain. Neither am I—nor am I a victim. We wanted to live different lifestyles. We had different priorities and values. We were in different stages of growth. I do wish him well on his journey, and I'm sure he's happier today, as am I.

CHAPTER 8

Falling into a Trauma-Bonded Relationship

I called him back

In January 2017, after separating from Chad and in the process of divorcing him, I met Joey at a workshop at the yoga studio near my new house. Joey was there with his sister Sarah. The three of us spoke a little at the workshop, then attended a sound healing that night at the same studio. Afterward, Joey and I started chatting in a Facebook group that had been set up for the workshop. I hadn't dated anyone since leaving Chad, and I was still unsure about the whole idea of it.

At first, Joey and I would only meet at the yoga studio for kundalini yoga, but it soon turned into dates and more time spent together outside yoga. When it came to showing me love and attention, Joey was the complete opposite of Chad. From the beginning, he love-bombed me constantly. I'd never met a man like him. He seemed too good to be true. And it turns out he was!

Joey was outgoing, funny, charismatic, attentive, romantic, and nurturing. This man actually wanted to spend time with me—a lot of it! It felt so foreign. He was a great cook and made me dinners. We had been officially seeing each other for three weeks when he cooked me a fancy lobster dinner served on nice china. We ate while watching the Super Bowl, and it was so much fun. He always put in the effort.

We also had yoga and spirituality in common. We even became certified in sound healing together. We were also both parents. Joey had a daughter from a previous marriage the same age as Westin who lived out of state. The fact that he didn't drink made him even more attractive to me. We had amazing chemistry together. Whether in person, on phone calls, or through text messages, Joey spoke to me in a way that made my self-confidence soar.

"You're beautiful."

"Thanks for cooking! Dinner tastes amazing."

"That's a really good idea."

"I want to see you every day!"

The first time Joey and I went out to an event together, I was shocked at how attentive he was. He never left my side the entire night. This was in sharp contrast to what I experienced in my marriage. When I went out to an event with Chad, I'd end up by myself because he'd leave me so he could work the room and drink.

After being starved for time and affection for two decades, I felt excited. I felt chosen. I felt seen. I felt desirable again.

At first, I ate it up because I needed and craved that external validation. Also, I'd found out Chad had already been dating a girl for quite a while, which made me more vulnerable to Joey's attention. I had been trying to heal from the separation and navigating the divorce, and it felt like a relief to meet someone who wanted me. I didn't have the tools to know how to be discerning in dating and to ask the right questions. I just dove in because it felt good.

But once I gained more distance from my marriage, Joey's attentiveness became suffocating. Slowly, I stopped needing anyone else's validation to be confident in myself. That process took several more years, and all the while Joey's insecurities chased us both through our relationship.

Despite Joey's good qualities, he was also overly attentive, clingy, and controlling. He had a jealous streak. If I didn't reply to a text message immediately, he thought something was wrong between us. If I didn't add a heart emoji to the end of a text message, he thought something was wrong between us. If I didn't laugh when he expected me to, he thought something was wrong between us. Looking back in my journals from that time, I notice I wrote about how fast he was moving the relationship. It didn't feel right to me, but again, I did not heed my intuition. As we dated, I also felt something was off with how many women he had lived with and dated since his divorce more than twelve years before. Red flag right there! His jealousy and controlling behavior were a pattern.

Toward the start of our relationship, my son had a soccer game, and both Chad and I had to be there to participate in parent-related activities. My mom and stepdad also decided to go. I felt awkward about Joey being part of that type of family gathering, so I didn't invite him. It was too soon in our relationship.

That morning, I told Joey, "I'll be at my son's game this afternoon. I'll call you after, okay?"

He was immediately offended. "Why don't you want me to be there?" Joey demanded. "What's going on? Does this mean we're not together?"

It took a while to smooth his ruffled feathers.

At the time, I didn't pick up on these red flags. All I saw was the gentleman. He'd open my car door for me. He'd open almost every door for me and insist I go through ahead of him. But if I walked too far ahead of him, that wasn't cool. If I didn't walk beside him or hold his hand, he'd get offended or think I was mad at him. He had all these little rules that, for Joey, signaled whether I loved him or not.

He accused me of cheating and was paranoid most of the time. I didn't know where this was coming from because I was a faithful partner to him, just as I was a faithful wife to Chad and my previous boyfriends. I value monogamy. I thought if I just kept reassuring him, and if I loved him enough, the behavior would stop. We had numerous conversations about how we both valued monogamy and were committed to each other.

When I started to realize how nutty this behavior was, it became clear that Joey had unresolved trauma from his childhood and dysfunction in his family, but he'd never gotten help for it. This caused him to constantly doubt and test his romantic partners' love for him.

Of course, I felt sorry for him. Who wouldn't? About three months into our relationship, Joey told me he was insecure. I thought it was because I was going through a divorce, but his insecurity never lessened, no matter how much time passed. Even after the divorce was finalized and we lived together, Joey would overreact to small things, like if I got home fifteen minutes later than he expected. He kept justifying his behavior as acceptable for a committed relationship. According to him, it wasn't controlling or overbearing; it was love. Joey showed up for me and was committed to me. He even gave me a diamond ring as a symbol of our commitment. Here I had a man that I felt was a partner, but he kept sabotaging the relationship with his chaotic behavior. It was a confusing time for me.

Joey's interest in guns also made me feel unsafe. He owned several guns, including an assault rifle. Even though he stored them in a gun safe, it freaked me out a bit. Joey knew I didn't like guns, but I never shared my opinion about his gun ownership specifically. That felt like it could go wrong fast. When we moved in together, he brought a gun out to the backyard while we were hanging out together.

"Why do you have that out?" I asked, my heart rate spiking.

He looked around. "Well, you never know what could happen. We don't know this neighborhood well yet."

Nothing was going to happen. We lived in North Scottsdale. There's not much crime in the area. He was just paranoid.

Joey never threatened me explicitly. Gradually, though, a low buzz of fear crept into my life. His mistrust scared me because I didn't know what he would do. I didn't know if he was going to snap one day. He had road rage problems and yelled into the phone at T-Mobile representatives when he felt they were taking advantage of him. More than once, he was verbally abusive to people on the phone.

During this time, I was growing, so I started trying to speak up for myself more and more. Whenever I brought up his behavior or tried to open a dialogue about our relationship, he would immediately get defensive or try to shift blame onto me. Sometimes he'd send me text messages that were so long I had to scroll down to read them all. Instead of taking accountability, he would blame my "hormones" or say I was messed up because of my divorce.

Because Joey could be so romantic and charming, his toxic behavior baffled me. His accusations were both confusing and chaotic. He was a bit like Dr. Jekyll and Mr. Hyde. Sometimes he'd present as a stable, attentive gentleman going out of his way to be helpful and nice. Aside from Joey's regular job, he was a Reiki master who helped people, but he also had another, much darker side. He was immature and couldn't emotionally regulate himself.

I began to feel trapped once again with a romantic partner who could not hold himself accountable for the life and relationship we were building together. Over time, it came to feel like I was walking on eggshells, not bringing up things I knew would upset him. Some days his paranoia and comments about how I spent my time and money made me withhold information about what I was doing or where I was going. I wasn't able to be authentically me for fear of his reaction or comments.

"Wow, it must be nice to have a fancy lunch," Joey would say.

"You're going for a massage? Lucky!"

"You must love getting your nails done."

Joey could play off these types of comments as not meaning anything, but they held an undertone of disapproval and judgment. I didn't eat at excessively fancy restaurants or get massages and manicures at exclusive spas. But his comments made me feel embarrassed about the way I lived my life and that I needed to change those spending habits . . . until I got sick of it. I began to see his attention as creepy. Joey even installed cameras inside my studio and our home. He claimed they were for security, but I know he also kept tabs on me.

One morning I had a client in the studio for a Pilates session. Alice was also a close friend, and I could tell immediately that she was upset.

"Are you okay?" I asked, worried. "Did something happen?"

"Do you mind if we get a coffee around the corner and talk?" Alice replied. "I don't think I'm up for my usual workout."

I'd already set my phone to vibrate, which I did for all my teaching sessions. About an hour into our chat at the coffee shop, I noticed my phone vibrating. It was Joey, and I decided to answer.

He yelled angrily into the phone. "Where are you? I've been trying to call you! Your car is at the studio, but you're not. I thought something bad had happened."

His reaction filled me with embarrassment. I'm sure my expression was uncomfortable to Alice. I explained to Joey where I was and what I was doing. He hung up.

Later, he kept questioning me. "Why did you have to go to a coffee shop? You have a coffee machine at your studio."

Not only did Joey have access to the cameras, but he was also able to locate my car via a tracking feature that connected it to his cell phone. I soon changed the settings so he couldn't track my car anymore. I recognize now the crazy control he was exhibiting and how I was shrinking into myself to stay with him.

One afternoon I ran into the husband of a friend while running errands around the corner from my studio. Jeremy, who I was friendly with, also worked in fitness.

"Oh, let me come look at your studio," he said cheerfully. "I'd love to see your setup."

The thought of bringing a male friend back to my studio, no matter how harmless and professional the context, freaked me out. Joey would see Jeremy on the cameras. I knew Joey would go bananas, so I made excuses to Jeremy. I was very conscious of how anything I did would affect Joey.

Joey also had physical issues from his job and had hurt his back in his twenties. He often played that up to get my attention and sympathy, which I ate up at first. While I felt sorry for him, I soon realized he liked playing the victim. He would accuse me of cheating, but he could talk to other women. He got jealous if I talked to another guy. He policed my Facebook posts and likes but got mad if I said anything about his. He took no responsibility for anything and went into defense mode as soon as I tried to have mature, adult conversations about our relationship.

He wasn't able to listen, so there could never be any resolution to our conflicts.

Before we moved in together, I knew that Joey used THC drops to cope with his back pain. It wasn't until after we began living together that I learned he also smoked marijuana, and that it made his paranoia worse. Yet I stayed in that relationship. I felt seen and wanted by him, and it took me a long while to understand that the extreme amount of attention he paid me stemmed from him wanting to monitor and control what I was doing and who I was seeing.

We went to counseling for eight months. Our counselor Stan tried to get Joey to share his feelings and open up. While he could see his behavior was hurtful, Joey continued to use his childhood trauma as justification. It was the reason, but he could not move past it to make changes.

Stan wanted to see Joey by himself, but he'd make excuses not to go.

"Oh well, he didn't take my insurance."

"I've got too much going on with work."

It seemed like Joey felt that simply going to counseling with me meant he was changing. While he made some changes, he still acted paranoid and immature.

Over the long 2021 Easter weekend, I flew up to visit Wyatt, who was living in Idaho. I texted and communicated with Joey every day. Easter morning, I texted him, *Happy Easter! I'm going to breakfast with Wyatt and his boss and wife. I'll call you when I get to the airport.*

Happy Easter, Joey texted back.

During breakfast, Joey called. I didn't answer since we were all at the table together.

Wyatt dropped me off at the airport. While I was going through security, Joey called again. More bad timing. I didn't answer then either.

At the gate, I called him back. Joey was livid. "Were you ever going to respond to me? Were you ever going to answer at all?"

"I texted you this morning and told you what was going on."

He snapped. "I didn't get any texts."

I took a screenshot of our messaging thread and sent it to him. Joey sent a screenshot back. My message to him had never gone through.

"Okay," I said. *Do you have to be upset, though?* I asked silently.

Joey started yelling at me, saying that he thought someone had kidnapped me.

I explained the bad timing of his calls. He didn't want to hear it. "No, it doesn't take that long to go through TSA."

Joey kept questioning and doubting me. That's what he'd been doing to me our entire relationship. Unreasonable. Untrusting. Accusatory.

Sitting at the gate, I pulled the phone away from my ear as he kept yelling at me.

I do not deserve this, I acknowledged. *I do not want to spend the rest of my life dealing with this.*

I interrupted, "Are you picking me up from the airport?"

"Yeah."

"I will see you then." I hung up.

Joey continued to send me messages until my flight touched down in Arizona.

I'm not doing this anymore, I decided.

When we got home, Joey said he had smoked some pot the night before and had bad dreams, which explained why he freaked out. I believed his childhood trauma was affecting his behavior, but I'd had enough. I just wanted him to get some real help, and I wanted to not be around his chaos any longer.

The process of us separating showed me Joey's true colors. I was the one who had bought the house we shared, and unfortunately, I had put him on the deed (BIG MISTAKE), so it became a shit show selling the house. He wanted to hold out for an overpriced amount, and I wanted to sell it quickly and move on. His inability to emotionally regulate came out with yelling and name calling. Before we put the house up for sale, I wanted him to move out. I was paying the mortgage, and he was paying the utilities and any improvements. This was the agreement we'd made before we moved in together. I offered to pay him all the money he put into the house, but he thought I was trying to cheat him. My intention was never to cheat him out of any money, but he was convinced I did. I just wanted it to be over and not fight him, so I agreed that we should sell the house. Because this happened during COVID, we were able to sell the house for a nice profit, as there was an influx of people wanting to move to Arizona. We both got all the money back we each put into the house. It was an amazing gift in a difficult situation. Thank you, Universe!

After we broke up, I moved into a new house and went on with my life. I felt lonely, angry at myself, and sad about Joey. I loved and cared for him deeply. Unlike in my marriage, our lifestyles and daily activities were intertwined, so the physical withdrawal was painful, almost like a detox.

About six months later, he sent me a text asking how I was doing. I was vulnerable and started talking to him again. He apologized, as usual, and I still held onto a shred of hope that maybe he had changed. I didn't tell my family and friends I was seeing him again. I was embarrassed. I'm even embarrassed as I write this because I got caught up again in the trauma-bond I had with him.

In a trauma-bonded relationship, the good behavior, emotions, and experiences are in constant tension with the bad. They flip-flop all the time, and that causes a person confusion. But you stay because you tell yourself the good outweighs the bad. You become anxious about which side of your partner—the good or the bad—is going to show up on any given day. You worry about how they're going to react to situations. It's a roller coaster. The highs and lows keep you chemically addicted.

Even though I let Joey back into my personal life, I was still cautious, only seeing him sporadically and not allowing him into life with my family. Soon, though, I realized his answer to healing was to do multiple ayahuasca ceremonies (he told me he did thirteen) as opposed to going to therapy. While I believe some healing can occur with ceremonies like these, I don't think they can replace the hard work of healing childhood trauma with a therapist. Joey also exhibited some of the same behaviors I saw when we lived together, like not being able to have a difficult conversation. Things had not changed, and I had to let that fantasy go. I was working hard to better myself by listening to experts like Life Coach Matthew Hussey and Dr. Ramani Durvasula on social media. Clearly this relationship with Joey wasn't going to work. The Universe soon gave me another tap on the shoulder to show me I needed to let go of it.

An impromptu conversation I had with Tessa, a woman in my yoga class, gave me the jolt to end our relationship. While I often saw Tessa at yoga, I didn't really know her. One day after class, she unexpectedly brought up dating in her fifties, and I chimed in with my own story. I told her about my situation with Joey. "Oh," she said, "I know Joey!" He'd gone to happy hour with Tessa and some of the yoga students, even though he didn't drink. "Joey told me he was on dating apps."

Tessa's revelation woke me up. Since I was only seeing *him*, I thought *he* was only seeing *me*. When I learned he was seeking out other people, I was livid and cut our relationship off completely. For years, Joey had constantly accused me of cheating, but he'd been hiding his dating life from me while we were trying to sort things out. While I thought he was "healing," he was actually speaking to other women and doing God knows what else. I was done.

During our relationship, Joey and I shared a membership to a resort in Mexico so we could go whenever we wanted for a discount. Long after we'd broken up and gone our separate ways, Joey called me. "I'm not using my reservation to Mexico this Thanksgiving," he said. "But if you want to buy it from me, you can. Or you could come with me, and you could fall in love with me again."

After I ended our relationship, Joey moved to the same neighborhood where I lived. That felt intentional, like he wanted to stay close to me and thought we would get back together. Everywhere I turned, it felt like he was there. Finally, I moved to a new neighborhood so I could create a new life.

Yet I still couldn't get away from him because Joey started going to the same yoga classes I attended. At first I tried my best to ignore it. I'd nod at him in passing, but that was it. When he kept coming, and it kept feeling like he was there for a reason, I confronted him.

"Do you need to talk to me or say something to me?" I asked. "You're coming to these classes now, and it feels intentional to be around me."

"Well, you know," Joey replied, "I sent you a birthday text and a Christmas text, and I never heard anything back from you."

"That's because I blocked you."

"Well, I just want you to be happy," he said. "Are you happy?"

Why is this any of your business? I thought, frustrated. *Why are you still hanging around my life?!*

I left that conversation, but he still came back to the yoga class. I tried again. "Really, what do you need to say to me to put this to bed? You never came to these classes before."

Joey apologized and spoke about how he was struggling in his relationship with his daughter and had hoped to see her soon. He talked about his continued "healing" ayahuasca ceremonies, and he verbally took responsibility for all his chaotic behavior in our relationship. Finally!

"That's nice of you," I said. "But it's not going to change anything."

Only acknowledging where he'd gone wrong wasn't going to fix the problem. All he really wanted was to regain my sympathy. He didn't accept that saying you have a problem isn't enough. Acknowledgment isn't the work. The work comes after. I also am clear that I need a sober partner moving forward. With his addiction to pot, he is not on my path.

Recently, I took a trip to Mexico with my best friend Paula. We went to the resort where Joey and I had a membership and had such a great time. Paula is so normal. She knows how to regulate her emotions. She's kind to everyone. I didn't have to worry that she would bring chaos into my life during the trip. I didn't have to worry how she would react to any missteps that happened.

On a trip to Mexico in the past, Joey accused me of looking at other men and cheating. He threatened to fly home. He was emotionally unregulated, and his accusations were unwarranted, so it felt nice to go there with my best friend and "reclaim" the resort with new positive, happy memories.

On that trip, I realized how far I'd come since ending my relationship with Joey. All relationships, whether platonic or romantic, take work. You have to nurture them. That work should uplift and empower both people in the relationship. It shouldn't tear either of you down.

When we were together, I looked up Joey's criminal history and discovered he had been arrested twice for domestic violence. I look back now with embarrassment, again, that I chose not to see this as a huge red flag. I reasoned that it had been more than twelve years ago, and he didn't act like that with me. I thought he had matured. I mistakenly believed he was nice, attentive, and kind. When I asked him about it, he blamed his "ex," but I didn't know if he meant his "ex-girlfriend" or his "ex-wife." Joey said, "My ex had a drinking problem." Part of me wanted to believe him, but I also knew he was not taking any accountability.

Yikes! Talk about being blind!

Red flags, problems, and patterns often seem obvious in hindsight, but that's often the way it is for people like me who haven't been in healthy, positive relationships before. I was going through my own slow, tough, hard-fought transformation during those years. For a period, Joey's romantic and nurturing qualities blinded me to the unhealthy aspects of his behavior. At the start of our relationship, I wasn't seeing a therapist. I wish I had been, but I'd stopped after separating from Chad. This was a big mistake. If I'd had a safe space to talk about my relationship with Joey, a trained therapist might have helped me see the red flags sooner.

My people-pleasing tendencies played a part as well, and I was overly empathetic to Joey. I wanted to make him happy, and I fell into the role of emotional caretaker, as so many women do in relationships. Instead of looking at my own trauma and taking care of myself, I took care of him because he'd had a traumatic childhood. Subconsciously, I also wanted to make my first relationship after my marriage work. I felt embarrassed and ashamed when it didn't.

What's wrong with me? I wondered. *How could this happen again? Why am I with emotionally immature men?*

As I worked on myself and gained agency, found my voice and confidence, and grew into the person I wanted to be, I could see that in both relationships, I did all the emotional labor—until I got tired of it. Once I'd gotten enough therapy and read enough psychology books to understand why I repeated this pattern, I replaced those questions with better ones: *What's my responsibility here? How do I not repeat this pattern and genuinely feel worthy of healthy love?*

In the end, my relationship with Joey wasn't a waste. I wish him well on his life journey also. I learned some big lessons from it. People will tell you who they are, but it doesn't always match who they show you they are. That's what you should trust and believe—the showing, not the telling. They may truly want to be the person they say they are, but they're still unable to do the hard work to actually be that person. It can be easy to get sucked into a fantasy story. It takes strength to quit the fantasy, accept reality, and build a life for yourself that's real. Finding real happiness is the best part about leaving behind a fantasy.

CHAPTER 9

When Professionals Fail and Parenthood Prevails

I did everything I could

My Bad Experiences with Counseling

I've gone to counseling and therapy many times as an adult. The first time was actually at age twenty-two when I broke up with Richard. I knew I needed some help getting through that breakup. I only saw her a few times, and she never dug into my family or how I grew up. A missed opportunity. Therapeutic interventions can be extremely valuable to an individual's healing and growth—and, overall, counseling has helped me in my journey. This doesn't mean that all the counseling I've received has been universally good. Sometimes it has delayed or set back my progress.

In Chapter 7, I discussed a bad experience I had with a counselor when my husband and I went to marriage counseling.

After Chad got a DWI in November 2005, I told Betsy, our counselor at the time, what had happened during a one-on-one session I had with her. She told me she couldn't talk about it with Chad in our couple's session unless he brought it up. At the time, I didn't know how ridiculous and wrong this was, and that Betsy absolutely could have brought up the topic with him first, or I could have. This was a huge, missed opportunity for Chad to finally address his drinking, childhood trauma, and the way he treated his family. It was also a missed opportunity for me. Betsy didn't give me a safe, supportive, and nonjudgmental space to help promote my self-awareness and personal growth. She didn't give me meaningful support during such a difficult time.

The stress and worry I dealt with in 2005 began at the beginning of the year, when my dad got his DWI in January. My worry for Dad—along with watching Chad's over-drinking and juggling all the problems in our marriage while being my sons' primary caregiver—left me feeling isolated and helpless. I couldn't figure out why I wasn't happy. In the first half of 2005, Chad and I were seeing a different counselor named Julie. Julie suggested I see my regular doctor about getting a prescription for an antidepressant.

I know Chad felt like I was the one with the problem because Julie wanted to put me on medication. He made me feel like I was incredibly messed up rather than just going through a completely understandable period of struggle. No one was helping me dig deeper into why I felt sad. So, after about six months, I went off the antidepressant. Instead, I began exercising even more to try to handle my sadness. Whether you take medication, go to counseling, or try different modalities to address your mental health struggles, whatever works for you is the right choice. Don't let anyone convince you otherwise. There is no one-size-fits-all.

While I don't regret taking an antidepressant, I don't think Julie guiding me toward medication ultimately helped me address the underlying issues I was struggling with, including the problems in my marriage with Chad. It felt a bit like being told, *Here, take this pill. I hope you feel better. See ya!*

Soon after, Julie moved away, and Betsy took over her clients. We had some friends who were seeing Betsy as well, and they found out she was going through her own divorce. When Chad learned this, he washed his hands of her. "Well, I'm not going to a counselor *for marriage counseling* who's getting divorced."

We didn't see Betsy again.

Years later, during an argument, Chad blurted out, "I'm going to cheat on you!" Again, the feeling of being unsafe enveloped my body. The threats to me and my safety silenced me again, and I went into "I've got to do everything I can to save my marriage and make my husband want me" mode. From a friend's referral, we started to see a new counselor. This counselor was even worse and again brushed off Chad's drinking issue. I refused to see him again after a handful of sessions when I realized he was not going to help us.

Unfortunately, none of the counselors we saw during this period (which spanned years!) genuinely tried to help me address the underlying causes of my struggles, Chad's addiction, or what was wrong in our marriage. No one enabled me to identify and solve the real problems in my life that were preventing me from growing, making positive changes, and leading the life I deserved. As a result, I couldn't figure out how to articulate what I wanted or needed. I knew so much was wrong in my life and marriage, but I didn't get any proper support. Ultimately, I was looking for a counselor to validate my feelings when I couldn't do it myself.

Not all counselors are made equal. You have to advocate for yourself when you feel you're not getting the help you need.

Being able to speak up and advocate for myself was one of the toughest skills I had to learn. But it was vital to me becoming the person I wanted to be and building the life I wanted to live.

I kept going through more cycles of unhappiness, yet I didn't want to give up. It wasn't until the beginning of 2016 that I had a breakthrough. Louise, my counselor at the time, recommended Chad and I see a marriage therapist, Daniel, who had a great reputation. It took me weeks to get us in to see him.

During our first appointment with Daniel, I was honest about how I was feeling and laid out all the struggles in our marriage. I finally felt heard. Because Daniel was a busy therapist, after that first appointment, I had already prebooked several upcoming appointments for us. The following week, on the morning of our second appointment, I asked Chad if he was going to meet me at Daniel's office.

"No," he replied dismissively. "I called and canceled all those appointments."

I was devastated. "What? You did *what*?"

"Yeah, I'm not going."

I couldn't believe it. Once the initial shock wore off, I couldn't deny the clear message this sent me. Chad wasn't willing to do any work on himself.

Later that afternoon, I got a surprising call from Daniel, who asked if I knew we had an appointment that day.

"My husband told me he called and canceled all of our appointments," I replied.

"It's still in my schedule," Daniel said, and I was stunned again. Either Chad had lied to me, or the appointment never got taken off Daniel's schedule.

"Do you want to come in and see me by yourself?" Daniel asked. "Oh, that's right, you already have a counselor."

"I do."

"Well, I'd just suggest you continue to see your counselor."

"Yes," I agreed wholeheartedly.

Like so many other times in our marriage, I avoided confronting Chad about whether he had lied to me about canceling the appointments or not. I did know, however, that by saying he had canceled them, he was telling me he had no intention of going back.

I realized, finally, that I had done everything I could—and decided I was done. In April 2016, I told Chad I was moving out.

His only reply was, "I'm going to have a great life."

It took a couple months for me to get everything organized and complete the move. I'm glad I got out.

Raising My Two Boys

My two amazing sons Westin and Wyatt are very precious to me. They are the lights of my life and the best things I've ever done. Because I'm adopted, they're also the first genetic family I've ever had. I'm very proud of them.

For their entire lives, I've worried that Westin and Wyatt would be affected by their family's history of alcoholism. Their father and paternal grandfather were both alcoholics. There's certainly a genetic component to addiction. Their maternal grandfather Glenn, though not biologically related to them, was also an alcoholic, and he was in their lives.

I raised my boys to be aware of the risks of drugs and alcohol. I was open about how my dad struggled with alcoholism and how he finally got sober. Dad also talked with the boys about his drinking problem and sobriety at the age of sixty-nine. As adults, Westin and Wyatt also now know that their paternal grandfather was a severe alcoholic and abuser before he got sober.

I wanted Westin and Wyatt to go to a preparatory high school because they drug tested students randomly. This gives students an external reason to say no if their peers pressure them to do something they don't want to. It also deters them with the thought of getting caught and its consequences. I talked with Westin and Wyatt often about the dangers of drinking and driving while high. My concern about substance use addiction led me to donate financially to Mothers Against Drunk Driving (MADD) for many years. I even joined the women's board of notMYkid, a nonprofit organization that provides high impact prevention education and early intervention programs for young people battling addiction.

Our kids were four and seven years old when Chad got his DWI. They didn't realize what had happened. Throughout their childhoods, Westin and Wyatt didn't see Chad drink a lot. He drank outside the home and came home after they went to bed. His binge drinking was a problem. Some alcoholics need to drink every day. Some over-drink on the weekends to cope with life and "unwind." In my own struggle with Chad's drinking, I avoided being fully honest with my kids. I thought I was protecting them. In reality, I was hiding and avoiding the truth.

I didn't want the same problems with addiction for my sons. I did everything I could to raise them right and model a healthy lifestyle for them. I'm sure they would say I've been preachy about the subject of addiction because I have been. The hurt I've had because of my experiences have made me passionate about the ill effects of alcohol and drugs. Of course, I will always worry about Westin and Wyatt. At some point, though, a mother has to have faith in her children and realize they are going to make their own decisions and live their own lives. All I can do is try to give them advice that may help them avoid the mistakes I made when I was their age. I tell them they aren't alone and there's no shame in getting help when they go through tough times.

Chad and I both grew up with so much dysfunction and silence in our families. So many people didn't know how to deal with what they were experiencing in a healthy way. All they could do was survive in whatever unhealthy way they could. It created entire generations of broken people. We deserved better when we were kids. Our sons deserve better today.

My hope is that the cycle of generational trauma, silence, and addiction passed down from parent to child in our families can be broken with our sons. Destructive behavior can reverberate through families across time, its consequences much larger than the person who's refusing to deal with their struggles ever imagines they will be. Change and growth is possible—not only within individuals who decide to improve their own lives, but also within families that recognize creating better lives for the next generation means more than putting a roof over their heads and food in their bellies. It means giving them the social and emotional tools they need to survive *and thrive* throughout life's hardships without turning to unhealthy or harmful behaviors, beliefs, lifestyles, or other coping mechanisms.

PART 3

Choosing Myself

CHAPTER 10

Empathy, Voice, and Independence

I am done being silenced

The Curse and Gift of Empathy

I'm either cursed or gifted to have empathy for people. Empathy is the ability to understand and share the feelings of another person. It involves putting yourself in someone else's shoes, recognizing their emotions, and responding with compassion. Empathy goes beyond simple awareness of another person's emotions; it requires a genuine connection and emotional response to their experiences.

One would think that having empathy is always valuable, but my empathy plays a significant role in why I've understood and maintained relationships with people who treat me poorly or even abuse me. It's hard to break the habit of empathizing with everyone around you, especially your loved ones, when it's so deeply ingrained in you.

In my marriage to Chad and relationship with Joey, I felt sorry for them. I thought that with enough love and care, I could help them so they could become the men I wanted and needed them to be for me. While I also thought we bonded over shared experiences (having children with Chad, for example, or sharing a love of spirituality and yoga with Joey), I ended up doing too much of the emotional labor in these relationships. That's my own dysfunction, and like many women, I felt more empathy for my partners and their traumatic experiences than I did for my own. People who have empathy often end up putting themselves second, third . . . or last. Empathy can become harmful and destructive when combined with insecurities or other hurts. If you don't learn how to treat yourself with compassion and care, then you can't have healthy relationships—with others or with yourself.

When you have empathy, it's easy and natural to justify poor behavior in other people. You tell yourself that they had such a terrible childhood, or they're just having a rotten day, or they don't mean it because you know who they really are deep down. The endless justifications become second nature and incredibly difficult to escape. When it gets out of hand or you don't maintain healthy boundaries, empathy can contribute to codependent behaviors. Highly empathetic people can overidentify with others' feelings and problems, leading them to absorb their emotional states and take on too much responsibility for their well-being. This can turn into codependent caregiving.

One way to break out of codependency and excusing another person's poor behavior is to turn that same narrative on yourself and consider the difference. For example, I also experienced some tough times in my childhood and adulthood, yet I don't treat other people badly. I began to ask myself, *Why am I excusing someone else's behavior when I'd never excuse the same behavior from myself?*

This is also your inner critic. You have to be aware of how harsh you're being with yourself. If I talked to other people the way I often thought about myself throughout my life, I wouldn't have any friends. Now that I'm aware of that inner critic, I catch myself and remind myself, *Okay, let's have some compassion and grace for yourself.* I'm still working hard on this one.

Having compassion for myself, setting boundaries, standing with my values, and learning about toxic people and relationships have been priorities of mine over the past two years. One thing I've especially learned more about is narcissism.

Narcissists are often attracted to people who have lots of empathy because they instinctually recognize the trait in them. They exploit it. Having too much empathy can be a trap. Like having to learn to break out of my codependency, it's often necessary to break out of the empathy trap more than once. I excused my husband's behavior for years, then ended up dating someone else who also treated me badly at times. I excused and justified Joey's behavior right up until I sat in an airport listening to him scream at me over the phone.

A big influence on my healing has been the work of Dr. Ramani Durvasula. Her YouTube videos and book, *It's Not You: Identifying and Healing from Narcissistic People,* have validated what I went through in my toxic relationships. One topic she discusses is how your background can make you vulnerable to narcissists and toxic people. As a child who grew up in an alcoholic family, I wanted to keep the peace and fix everything. Dr. Ramani writes, "You may also be conflict averse, a pattern we often see as a part of trauma bonding. Fixers may often capitulate to what the narcissistic person wants and avoid setting boundaries because of tension and conflict that would come from those boundaries."[1]

This was definitely my problem: trying to fix and avoiding setting boundaries to dodge conflict.

You can't make someone better who doesn't want to get better. In most of my romantic relationships, I didn't understand this. I wasn't mature enough to realize that I'm responsible only for my actions and choices. In my marriage, I was responsible for not enabling Chad's drinking or his poor treatment of me—but that's it. Eventually, though, I learned. Then I had to learn it again with Joey, who didn't want to work on his own codependency issues and insecurities. The growth and maturity process is a learning curve that goes up and down.

For years, my dad didn't want to address his drinking—until the day he did. His DWI made him see the severity of his problem; then change came from within him. Change has to come from within. This doesn't mean we all have to do it all by ourselves without any support. Asking for help doesn't signal weakness or take away from a person's independence. It's a sign of strength. But no one can force help on someone else.

Today I always come back to the mantra, "You can't fix yourself by fixing someone else." You have to stay in your own lane. You have to have empathy for yourself, work on yourself, and focus on fixing yourself. I'm continuing to work on having difficult conversations and not being afraid of displeasing or angering people. I am learning to set boundaries and be discerning about who I let into my life and energy.

---

[1] Ramani Durvasula, *It's Not You: Identifying and Healing from Narcissistic People* (Penguin Random House, 2024), 141.

Finding Our Voices as Women

For a long time, even when it felt like I did have a voice, I always backed down. If I started to confront someone and they were aggressive with me or dismissed my feelings, I didn't push back. I didn't have the tools or emotional awareness to realize I froze every time someone came at me with aggression and conflict. I've come a long way, but I'm still learning how to stand up for myself and not simply accept when someone tries to ignore my feelings or my understanding of what happened. You have to stick to what you know to be true. You can't bottle up your sadness, anger, and fear forever. It's destructive.

Slowly I learned how to choose and prioritize myself and my own needs and wants over other people. Many women have to learn to do this intentionally because we're conditioned from the time we're young to put other people first.

I grew up about an hour from Disney World in Florida, and my family visited often. My favorite ride as a child was "It's a Small World." I was enamored with all the themes from the different countries and loved the "It's a Small World" song. That was the first spiritual encounter of oneness that resonated with me. Dad used to tell the story of when I was there with him at about five years old. We were standing in line for a ride when a man walked up and got in line in front of us.

I said, "Hey, you can't cut in line!"

The man laughed. "Pipe down, shortcake."

It turned out he was joining his wife in line where she was standing in front of us. But from my perspective as a child, this man was cutting in line. Looking back, I see how he silenced me with his mocking dismissal. He could've said, "Oh, I'm here with my wife, and she was saving my spot." Instead he told a little girl to be quiet.

How many times—and in how many big and small ways—are girls and women told to pipe down, be silent, or shut up?

I've been told to shut up plenty of times and in plenty of ways. Sometimes when I've expressed my opinion, being shut up sounded like, "This isn't about you." When I've disagreed with someone, I've been told I was "argumentative."

The time my husband wrapped his hands around my neck and choked me he could have seriously injured or killed me. But since he didn't remember what he'd done (or wouldn't acknowledge it), and my friend didn't say anything when I told her, I never dealt with it. I was a woman who had been silenced, denied, and dismissed by this type of violence and by being called a "buzzkill" and a "Debbie Downer." When I found drugs in Richard's bedroom, he shoved me against a door for trying to talk to him about it.

I am done being silenced and controlled.

My story is familiar to most women because too many of us are silenced and controlled. We are raised to be "nice" girls, to play small, to be amiable, to be accommodating. I used to think my life was about others. It never occurred to me to view my life as being just for me.

I grew up being told what to do instead of being asked my opinion or what I thought. I felt I had no choice or say in many matters. From my parents and other adults, I heard, "Do as you're told," and "This is how it is." I was talked *at* and not *with*. In my marriage, I heard, "This is how it is," or "This is what I'm doing." My opinions, my desires, and my feelings were dismissed.

The Good and Bad Sides of Independence

Growing up, I had to be very independent. Both my parents worked. My mom was a math teacher and instilled in me and my sister the importance of doing well in school. I wasn't super smart, but I knew how to study, and I could learn quickly. I always did my homework and excelled at schoolwork. I knew if I did this, I'd be accepted and praised by my parents and teachers. I tried to be perfect so I wouldn't upset my mom. I never wanted to be the center of attention or praised in front of other people, though. I feared kids my age wouldn't like me if I was given too much attention. Even during this part of my life, and in the face of my own accomplishments, I learned how to stay small and unseen.

Being independent as a child often felt lonely. I had to navigate feelings and puberty on my own. I had questions about boys, periods, and other normal things that girls need to talk about with a parent, guardian, or appropriate mentor. I never had that with my mom. She seemed too busy and upset with my dad to be bothered. I never felt I could approach her and talk about these things, so I kept them to myself and figured it out alone. That's how I've operated most of my life.

At fifty-five years old, I've finally figured out that I'm able—and allowed—to keep myself safe. I create my own safety with my independence, and I don't have to be around anyone who makes me feel unsafe. Toxic people don't get my time anymore. I have empathy and compassion for others, but I don't put them before my own safety, empathy, and compassion for myself.

I've been on a journey to find the true, healthy independence that I deserve as an adult woman. I've depleted myself trying to get people I love to do better and be better, and I realize now that's not my job. My job is to make myself better. This doesn't mean not caring for my family or friends. It *does* mean letting people figure out their own path. Sometimes that means they'll need to crash first. I can say to them, "I'm sorry you're having a hard time and hurting." I can sit and listen and let that be it.

Do you see the good and bad sides of independence? Children aren't meant to be fully independent. It stunts their social and emotional development. They depend on the adults around them; that's the way it's supposed to be. Too much independence in childhood can lead to codependence in adulthood. Being independent as an adult isn't a rejection of other people, the love they have for you, or the positive role they can play in your life. Healthy independence in adulthood means first being able to stand on your own two feet, then deciding who and what you let into your life. It also means being able to ask for help when you need it and not feeling like you need to have everything together all the time.

Because I spent so much time looking for love and validation outside myself, through other people or accomplishments in school or work, the codependent relationships I found myself in seemed normal, even as I struggled with unhappiness, resentment, and anger. I gravitated toward men with trauma in their backgrounds, which made them more susceptible to addiction and toxic behaviors. The first step to breaking out of codependency and gaining independence as an adult is recognizing that you can create your own safety, joy, and change. Then you can start to act.

You can identify the specific codependent behaviors you exhibit, define what you're willing and unwilling to do for others, and prioritize your self-care and self-worth. You can challenge negative thought patterns, practice self-reflection like journaling and mindfulness, and seek professional help and expertise in books, therapy, support groups, workshops, and more. You can learn to communicate effectively with others, expressing your needs and feelings openly and honestly. You can take small steps and big steps, paying attention to the gradual change you see and having patience with yourself. You can build a support network to keep yourself accountable, celebrate your wins, and pick yourself up when you have a setback. You *can* develop healthy relationships without sacrificing your independence.

CHAPTER 11

My Spiritual Path and "Good Girl" Conditioning

I belong to me

When I was a little girl, I said a prayer every night before going to sleep:

"Now I lay me down to sleep,

I pray the Lord my soul to keep,

If I should die before I wake,

I pray the Lord my soul to take.

God bless Mom, Dad, Heather, and everyone else in the world."

I agonized over who to add to the list after my sister. The thought of missing someone important upset me, so I added the "everyone else" clause to make sure no one would be left out. Even from that early age, the spiritual side of me knew that we are all one. I always struggled with the teaching that people outside my religion would go to hell. Even as a young girl I thought it didn't make sense that because someone grew up in a different county and lived by a different religion that God would send them to hell. In all honesty, I think hell is found here on earth in the hatred, violence, and separation that pulls us apart. Heaven, according to *A Course in Miracles*, is the awareness of our perfect oneness.

I've walked a winding spiritual path. I grew up attending church and Sunday school. At one point in time, I knew every book of the Bible and studied them. When we moved to Washington state from Florida, my mom, sister, and I began attending a Baptist church. My interest waned around eleventh grade, and my attendance became much more sporadic. For a ten-year period starting in college, I didn't go to church at all. Then, in 1997, the same year I had Westin at twenty-eight, I began attending a Methodist church in Arizona. I became involved and went there regularly until 2014. I joined the praise band and volunteered my time, participating in the congregation's community work. I brought my boys with me, and Chad came casually. My boys also went to a Lutheran elementary school—Westin from grades three to eight and Wyatt from kindergarten to grade eight. From there, they both went to a Catholic high school.

Religion was always around us. I have mixed feelings about the role religion played in my childhood and development. On the one hand, the Ten Commandments were drilled into me and made me value treating everyone with kindness. Even at a young age, I had a firm belief in justice, equality, and fairness for all. On the other hand, religious training pushed my need to please everyone over the top. I had to be a good girl. I had to be nice. I had to make sure everyone was taken care of, even if it meant I had to do all the work alone. It certainly contributed to my inability to stand up for myself and put my own self-care first.

Thank goodness that gal is fucking long gone.

That mindset wasn't healthy. It wouldn't be healthy for anyone, but especially for girls and women who are taught to be submissive and only take care of others rather than themselves. The Bible teaches us to treat others the way we would like to be treated, yet many people who go to church on Sundays don't practice this and are hypocrites. There's a fine line between treating everyone fairly and forgetting to treat yourself that way too. Dysfunction, codependency, abuse, and other unhealthy relationship dynamics thrive when that line is crossed.

My religious upbringing also exacerbated the silence surrounding the tough topics that my family didn't discuss, like my dad's alcoholism and the lack of opportunity I had to develop a strong identity and follow my intuition. The religious doctrine taught to me was very much, "This is the way it is." If someone did *these* things, they were a good person. If they did *those* things, they were a bad person. The doctrine was black and white.

As a result of my religious training, I grew up believing God was watching me. If I didn't behave like a good girl, He would punish me, and I'd go to hell. Like so many other teenagers, I snuck out of the house to drink and have fun with my friends when I was fifteen years old. Yet I couldn't shake the feeling, *I'm a bad kid.*

I was never a bad kid, though. I didn't act out. I got high grades. I didn't get in trouble at school. I tried hard not to worry or upset my parents.

The one time I used a swear word in front of my dad, he said, "Good girls don't talk like that." I rolled my eyes and moved on, but I never swore in front of him again. Almost every girl goes through conditioning like this by their parents, their religious communities, and our patriarchal society. The conditioning I received didn't take place through abuse or fundamentalist codes of behavior, but make no mistake, this was conditioning plain and simple—and almost every girl goes through it.

When I was thirteen years old, I had a sleepover with some of my girlfriends. We had a fantastic time taking photos with each other. This was back when cameras used film, and you had to pay to have it developed. Well, when Mom picked up the developed film from the store, she saw that in some of the photos, we'd stuffed balloons down our shirts (like boobs).

She got upset. "I'm disappointed in your pictures here, Laura," she said. "This is ugly behavior."

This is ugly behavior.

It wasn't only my behavior that I came to see as ugly. As so many other girls go through, I thought my looks and body were ugly. While I was athletic—I played softball and did gymnastics—and didn't think too much about my weight, I also didn't fit the conventional beauty mold. I didn't see myself physically represented in TV, movies, and magazines. I was short, muscular, and had Italian features. In school, my classmates threw hurtful comments at me about my big nose and the beauty marks on my face, which affected how I saw myself.

I never had anyone I felt I could talk to about this. Heather was conventionally pretty, so although we were close in other ways, I was never comfortable talking to her about my looks. My dad was an absent father, and my mom didn't create an environment where we could talk about puberty, normal body changes, and sexuality. My mom's disconnection from her own body and her disapproval of me even being funny about it, made me feel shame about my own changing body and my looks. We didn't need to talk about how I looked, especially not how I looked different from my adoptive family members. This lack of any open discussion about my appearance, coupled with not being able to physically identify with anyone in my family, made me feel ugly.

Even though my mother told me I was pretty, I never believed it inside myself.

Mom also didn't have the highest self-esteem and often put down her own physical appearance and intellect—despite having a master's degree in mathematics and working as a math teacher, then a computer programmer for Boeing. She never spoke well about herself, and that self-denigration got programmed into me.

I'm not blaming my mom. She was a product of her generation and family. As the fourth of six siblings, she didn't get much attention growing up. In large families like that, at that time children were thought to be doing well if their basic needs were being provided for, and that was it. Mental health awareness and open conversation about tough topics weren't on anyone's radar. While the Internet and social media have wreaked havoc on young people in many ways, they have also helped educate people about mental illness, abuse, and how and where to get help—even online therapy.

Growing up without anyone to talk to about all this, I didn't know that most adolescents felt the same way, and I was normal. I felt anything but normal and really lost in my identity. If I could go back in time, I would tell myself, "You are normal. All the changes and feelings you're experiencing are absolutely natural. Stop comparing yourself to others and quit looking at magazines and TV. It's all airbrushed."

I love what Dr. Clarissa Pinkola Estés writes about women and their body images in *Women Who Run with the Wolves*:

Harsh judgements about body acceptability create a nation of hunched over tall girls, short women on stilts, women of size dressed as though in mourning, very slender women trying to puff themselves out like adders and various other women in hiding. Destroying a woman's instinctive affiliation with her natural body cheats her of confidence. It causes her to perseverate about whether she is a good enough person or not, and bases her self-worth on how she looks instead of who she is. It pressures her to use up her energy worrying about how much food she consumes, the readings on the scale and tape measure. It keeps her preoccupied, colors everything she does, plans, and anticipates. It is unthinkable in the instinctive world that a woman should live preoccupied by appearance this way.[2]

A good girl doesn't drink or smoke, doesn't swear, and doesn't explore her body. She goes to church every Sunday, obeys her parents, obsesses over her looks, and only thinks about sex after marriage. She gets good grades, never acts out, and dresses nicely. She grows up and gets a strong education, gets married, and has children while building a career. She does everything—and she never complains. She puts everyone else before herself—and still she never complains.

So much of this messaging was delivered to girls like me implicitly and rarely stated directly, but the conditioning effectively got me and other girls to internalize these messages and beliefs about good and bad behavior. I thought because I did not follow all these "rules" that I was inherently bad.

This is ugly behavior.

Because there were so many rules and conditions about how I was supposed to behave, I wasn't free to express myself. That lack of freedom impacted my ability to follow my gut and stand up for myself. I didn't have any confidence.

---

[2] Clarissa Pinkola Estés, *Women Who Run with the Wolves: Myths and Stories of the Wild Woman Archetype* (Ballantine Books, 1996), 216.

When we were in high school, a boy said to my sister Heather, "Oh, your sister is really stuck up."

Heather didn't understand. "What? No, she's not! Like, what are you talking about? She's just really shy."

When you're a teenager, you don't know who you are. You struggle with the changes your body is going through and where you fit into the world and with your peers, as well as what education and career choices you're going to make. Add to those normal teenage struggles all these other factors—adoption, family dysfunction, religious upbringing, a patriarchal society—and my intuition became incredibly impaired. I was quiet, reserved, and unsure of myself; I didn't know how to trust myself. All I knew was how to be a "good girl."

Let's take a look at how this "good girl" conditioning has followed me through my entire life by skipping ahead to my most recent romantic relationship with Joey. About seven or eight months into dating, we went to a music event together. While there, I saw the ex-husband of a woman I know named Jackie.

I pointed out the ex-husband to Joey. "Hey, his ex-wife Jackie is going to be on the same notMYkid women's board of directors that I was on." I was just making conversation.

A week or so later, I found out that Joey had friended Jackie on Facebook. He had been showing me something on his Facebook page when the new friend connection popped up.

Jackie was a very attractive single woman—so attractive that she appeared in *Sports Illustrated*. I brought it up with Joey. "If we're in a relationship, this is not okay. Why would you do that?" She hadn't been at the music event. She was a complete stranger to him.

It wasn't that I was jealous. It was that it felt like Joey was disrespecting the relationship we were building. It made me question whether he and I had different views about what we had together and what we each wanted.

Joey got really mad. His reaction was ridiculously out of proportion with the calm, open conversation I thought we could have.

The next day I still wanted to talk about it. We went to a restaurant to have breakfast. While we were there, I said, "I would really like to talk about this." I was trying to use my voice and talk things out in this relationship in hopes of not repeating the noncommunicative dynamics of my marriage.

Joey set down his fork and knife. "You know what? I've lost my appetite. I don't want to eat anymore. I told you. I don't want to talk about this anymore."

I sat there while Joey raised his voice, visibly angry, then refused to talk to me. He shut down because I wanted to have a difficult conversation. All I could think was, *Oh my gosh, what is happening right now?*

All my "good girl" conditioning kicked in. I sat quietly and didn't argue back. I didn't make a scene like him. I didn't point out how hypocritical he was being. Joey got jealous if I so much as spoke platonically with another man, yet he could friend Jackie on Facebook. The double standard was ludicrous.

We packed up our leftovers, got in the car, and I drove him home. "That was embarrassing," I said.

I dropped him off and left.

I can't believe I stayed with Joey, but my "good girl" conditioning, high empathy, and codependency allowed me to rationalize it all away. Afterward, Joey went out of his way to apologize. He went overboard, love-bombing me hard with flowers, a massage, dinner, and attention. I got sucked back in, forgave him, and we never resolved the issue. It showed me that I wasn't safe bringing up anything that might upset him. I should have trusted my intuition. My gut was telling me that he was full of it, but I didn't listen. I didn't trust myself that I was strong enough to *not* be in a romantic relationship. I still needed the validation that came from being with someone.

I spent my entire life trying to be seen by boys and men, wanting to be loved and praised by my mom and teachers, wanting my dad to love me and give me attention, wanting to know where I came from and who I belonged to. When really . . . I belong to me. I'm the only person who can keep me truly safe and loved.

Once I started trying to grow and learned I needed to heal if I was ever going to be the person I wanted to be, the role of religion in my life shifted into spirituality. This started while I was still married to Chad. I became a spiritual seeker. It happened slowly over time. It involved both intentional spiritual pursuits and other efforts to find help, support, and opportunities to grow. I went to therapy on my own (and still do) and did eye movement desensitization and reprocessing (EMDR) to treat PTSD. I attended Al-Anon, a support program for people whose lives have been affected by someone else's drinking. I took up yoga and meditation.

I devoured books on spirituality and self-help by authors like Marianne Williamson, Eckhart Tolle, Byron Katie, and Elizabeth Lesser. I read books about feminism, like the works of feminist activist and scholar Bell Hooks. I read books about how to think differently and how to heal childhood trauma and relationships. Dr. Wayne Dyer's work was quite influential to me. He spoke at an annual self-help conference called Celebrate Your Life that I went to many times. I used to play his CDs in the car when my kids were in junior high, much to their eye rolls. I also studied *A Course in Miracles* on my own and as part of a study group at New Vision Center, a spiritual center in Arizona.

Starting in 2022, I realized I needed to take a harder look at the patterns in my behavior and mindset and try something new to help me change. I participated in a retreat led by Life Coach Matthew Hussey. I was so impressed by the retreat that I joined his private coaching group, Club 320. His coaching led me to take a deeper look at my pattern of dating men with chemical addictions and how to raise my standards, set boundaries, and level up my self-worth. I've made new friends and expanded out of my comfort zone since working with him and his team. The many key phrases and mantras I've learned from Hussey's work, like "Follow your path, not your feelings," have helped me immensely.

In *Love Life: How to Raise Your Standards, Find Your Person, and Live Happily (No Matter What)*, Hussey writes, "If we are serious about the path we've chosen—and we should be, since we already know where the previous paths went wrong—we will say no to things that only provide short-term comfort or excitement."[3] When Joey was hanging around me wanting to get back together, this quote helped keep me on track with my values and path. I am deeply grateful for Hussey's guidance and wisdom.

By becoming a spiritual seeker, I prioritized finding personal answers, understanding more about myself, and learning how we're all connected. "One love" has always resonated with me on a deep level. Nobody is better than anybody else. Nobody deserves to be treated as less than anybody else, including me. I shifted to seeing God as all loving instead of a judge waiting to condemn me to hell for "misbehaving." I now see all of us as brothers and sisters, and the message is we are to love each other, no matter our gender, race, ethnicity, religion, or sexual preference. It's a simple message, yet it's not easy to just love, especially with those who push our buttons. I believe we can love someone from afar but not want to have them in our lives. Simply wish them well

---

[3] Matthew Hussey, *Love Life: How to Raise Your Standards, Find Your Person, and Live Happily (No Matter What)* (Harper, 2024), 108.

and move on. I truly believe our purpose in life is to be a loving presence in the world.

There's true beauty in the interconnectedness of the world. Love can be a guiding force when we intentionally pay attention to it. Transformation is possible. I focused on figuring out how to live a life from healthy love, not out of fear or codependency. If you have compassion for other people, but you don't have compassion for yourself, the relationships you build will never be truly healthy. I was always hard on myself and lacked self-compassion. I've had to learn how to give myself grace. I easily gave compassion to others, and often when I shouldn't have, but I only rarely gave it to myself.

My spiritual path led me to more self-acceptance. I developed a view of oneness and connectedness with humanity, which made me feel a part of something bigger than myself. I feel that my existence is part of a divine plan of my spirit. Thinking of our spirit having a human experience in a body that's just a temporary vessel for the spirit has also helped me accept my physical body, which will age and eventually die. My spirit, however, is ever-present and will live on because it belongs to the Universe, like all of us, and that connects every one of us to each other. I came from Divine Source, not just from my biological parents.

Today, as a woman in my fifties who has gone through menopause, I feel more in tune with my body than ever and know when something is off. I take care of myself but don't obsess over my appearance. I want to look put together for myself, not anyone else, and I take care of myself for my own longevity. I'm doing everything I can to age with grace but also embrace changes. All the wrinkles, stretch marks, and "fun spots," as I call them, come with wonderful memories of a life well-lived.

Each of us walk our own religious and spiritual paths. Religion and spirituality do not have to be an "either/or" choice.

They can be a "both/and" choice. It's entirely possible to take teachings, lessons, and tools from both religion and spirituality and put them together in a way that works for you. Self-growth comes when you decide what works and what doesn't work for you in the religious and spiritual path you choose, as well as in your relationships, the boundaries you set, and the lifestyle you choose. It's okay when someone in your life or a path you've been walking doesn't meet the standards you set for yourself anymore. Walk away. Find a new path. Don't keep suffering. You don't deserve it. You get to choose.

Ultimately, it doesn't matter what specific religious or spiritual path works for you and serves the person you want to be. The farther you walk down the path you choose with intention and love, the wiser you will become. This is especially true for every "good girl" out there who wants to grow into the healthiest version of themselves.

CHAPTER 12

Growing Identity and Intuition

I became the woman I deserve to be

It wasn't until I grew into the person I was meant to be that I discovered the essential role intuition plays in a woman's life. Intuition is your sense of deep knowing about what is real, true, or meaningful, separate from external explanation or conscious reasoning. It's a quick, automatic grasp of what's really going on, or what you really have to do. You get a gut feeling inside that something occurring in your life is either good or bad for you. Maybe your intuition is telling you that something is off, and you need to stay away from someone. Maybe your intuition is telling you that you absolutely have to take a leap into the unknown in your professional life because it may be the best thing for you. Your intuition is a vital part of your own internal voice.

I've learned quite a bit about intuition, especially women's intuition, from Dr. Clarissa Pinkola Estés. In *Women Who Run with the Wolves*, she writes:

> When a woman's instinctual nature is strong, she intuitively recognizes the innate predator by scent, sight, and hearing . . . anticipates its presence, hears it approaching, and takes steps to turn it away. In the instinct-injured woman, the predator is upon her before she registers its presence, for her listening, her knowing and her apprehension is impaired—mainly by introjects which exhort her to be nice, to behave, and especially to be blind to being misused.[4]

For most of my life, I was an instinct-injured woman. So many aspects of my life made me doubt my own intuition and voice. My adoption. My religious upbringing and "good girl" conditioning. My family dysfunction. My codependent romantic relationships and the toxic behavior I endured. For a long time, these all combined to severely impair my intuition. It was drowned out by other, louder messages coming at me from outside myself. All that messaging molded me into a good girl, a good woman, a good wife, a good mother—but none of that left any space for me to discover and develop the parts of my identity that were uniquely *me*. I was always only *Laura for someone else.*

Eventually, something has to give. You can either break, or you can have a breakthrough. For me, I had breakthroughs once I started hearing my intuition. Over time those breakthroughs added up—not all at once, but in slow, small drips that helped me learn, grow, and empower myself.

---

[4] Pinkola Estés, *Women Who Run with the Wolves*, 73.

I became the woman I deserve to be. I became *Laura for me and only me*.

My Intuition was Proved Right

When your intuition is proved right, it's like you're connected directly to the world around you. It's like you can see beneath its surface in a way few others close to you can. For someone like me, who spent so long unable to tap into my intuition, these times in my growth are especially meaningful—in retrospect. Often you need your intuition the most during moments and experiences that are difficult, scary, or heartbreaking. The deeper meaning they hold only becomes clear later.

One of the turning points in my life, when I first began to discover my intuition, or perhaps develop trust in it, was the time my dad got his DWI.

Because I spent so much of my life feeling like I didn't know who I was and couldn't trust myself, many of my actions and choices were made for self-preservation. This became especially apparent during conflicts. I didn't know how to handle conflict because healthy conflict resolution had never been modeled for me. I was taught that you just move on and stuff the feelings down. You may be resentful, but that should also be stuffed down.

For so long I thought other people's hurtful or dysfunctional behavior should be ignored, especially if they deny or dismiss it. It's an elephant in the room, and the elephant should be ignored at all costs. Doing this put other people's feelings and comfort above my own. I dismissed my own needs to make them feel better. That was unhealthy. Not expressing myself as authentically as possible also didn't serve the other person well. It wasn't healthy for anyone.

When my dad got his DWI, it confirmed for me that I had been right as a child that something in our household had been terribly wrong. He had a real problem. The sense of wrongness I'd carried for so much of my childhood had been right all along.

My intuition had been telling me the truth.

When my dad visited for Christmas a few weeks before getting his DWI, I finally took a stand after he hurt and vomited on himself after getting so drunk he couldn't stand up properly. I stopped dismissing what I knew in my heart to be true. I told him he needed help—even though he wouldn't hear it—and I told him he couldn't drink while he was in my home. I didn't have to accept his behavior or the elephant that had been in the room with us for my entire life.

I didn't speak up many times throughout my life and my relationship with my husband. While I could confront Dad at that point, I was still unable to confront my husband about his drinking. That growth would take several more years of hard work.

A second example of my intuition being proved right occurred after my relationship with Joey ended. This is not the second time in my whole life when my intuition helped me. Rather, it is one of the most recent moments in time that I know would have ended badly and set my growth back terribly had I ignored my intuition.

I've realized that I sought out love in others in search of love for myself. It seems like I had boyfriend after boyfriend until I was twenty-three years old, when I finally took a short break. Then I met my now ex-husband, Chad. I was with him for the next twenty-three years. When we separated, I took a break before meeting my now ex-boyfriend, Joey.

2023 was a year of extreme grief for me and the hardest time mentally in my life. I spent time sitting in the grief of my dad's death, losing a trauma-bonded relationship, and closing my business. All the external validation I'd had for my own self-worth was gone, and it was time for me to learn to validate myself.

For months I cried myself to sleep. I had to fight with myself not to contact Joey, as he was always a nurturer. It would've been easy to text or call him for comfort. He lived less than ten minutes from me. His mother died five weeks after my dad died. His sister was the one who told me their mother died, as I still kept in occasional touch with her. I kept thinking about him and wondering how he was. I felt sorry for both of us, losing a parent and grieving. And this is how a trauma-bond plays out. You still have empathy for someone who has done you harm because you romanticize the good and forget the bad. I did not contact him, though, thanks to Matthew Hussey and Dr. Ramani. I listened to them almost every day to remind me of my worth.

In May 2023 I began to experience marked dizziness and fatigue. I did hot yoga frequently and thought I was dehydrated, so I backed off those classes. When the symptoms didn't subside, I went to my naturopath and had blood work done, along with tests on my heart. I was diagnosed with adrenal fatigue, which can be caused by chronic emotional stress. I'd been smart to close my business. After working six days a week, grieving my dad's death, and the final breakup from Joey, my body was at a breaking point. It needed rest. I took five months to fully heal by slowing my life down and giving myself time to heal.

I journaled and meditated daily, went to therapy, gently exercised, and found a new rhythm for myself. I discovered cranial sacral massage, which helped my nervous system calm down. I finally had time to truly focus on myself.

That July, Joey sent me a text message asking how I was. He started sending old pictures of us together too. Something about the timing felt strange. My intuition kicked in, and even though I didn't follow him on social media any longer, I decided to look at his Instagram posts. Sure enough, Joey's feed was full of photos of him and a gorgeous woman that were taken just two weeks prior. They went to all the same restaurants and places that he and I used to go to together. It made me sick. It turned out Joey started dating someone new not long after his mother died. They were together for three or four months, and he messaged me after the relationship ended. He was hitting me up because they broke up, and he was probably looking for attention (sex, sympathy, companionship).

I got so angry. There I was in a pit of grief and still feeling sorry for him, and he was out pulling the same moves on another casualty of his love-bombing. I'm grateful my intuition had developed enough to recognize his text message as a potential red flag and that I'd grown enough to know I should listen to my gut. I knew what was really going on before I could explain it. My personal growth kept me from romanticizing the relationship and falling back into the trap.

Thanks to Matthew Hussey's teachings, one thing I've done to help me heal is to place positive emotional buttons around my house that trigger a strong emotional response. For example, I bought a large canvas picture of a buffalo and put it in my bedroom so I see it when I go to bed and wake up because buffalo instinctively walk *into* rather than *away from* a storm, making their actual time experiencing a storm shorter. When I see this picture, it helps me take difficult things—like feeling the grief of losing my father and our relationship—and deal with them head on, instead of avoiding them.

I also have numerous lotus flowers in my house. From my love of yoga, I found the phrase "no mud, no lotus," which refers to how lotus flowers rise from mud without stains, blooming at the break of day and returning to the murky water each evening. These beautiful flowers symbolize strength, resilience, and rebirth, reminding me that you can thrive and bloom even in the most trying conditions.

CHAPTER 13

Metamorphosis from Avoidance to Acceptance

I am fully whole just as I am

Keeping Busy to Avoid the Real Issues

Personal growth isn't possible if you don't acknowledge there's a problem and identify, specifically, what you need to change. So many of us are unable to confront our real issues, let alone do something positive and healing about them. Sometimes we don't have the tools and knowledge to help us. Sometimes we don't have the emotional maturity. And sometimes we don't have the bravery.

Chad always had an "I do what I want to do" attitude. He had plenty going on: his businesses, his volunteer and philanthropy work, and his expensive status symbol hobbies. He built a life where he felt important precisely *because* he was busy all the time. That "busyness" did not include me. In truth, he kept busy to avoid his real issues. Just like I spent too much time keeping busy to avoid dealing with the dysfunction in our marriage. Just like my mom spent too much time keeping busy when she was married to my alcoholic dad.

In my thirties and early forties, I peeled off a layer of the onion that was our dysfunctional marriage when I stopped viewing Chad through rose-colored glasses and realized he was never going to be a true partner to me. But I was still committed to finding a way to live within the constraints of our relationship dynamics. It was easy to keep my head down and stay busy. We had two young sons who needed raising, and I could follow my own pursuits. I could run the household without a true partnership, more like a project manager than a member of a loving marriage. I got my Personal Trainer and Pilates Certifications, owned a small business, and did my own volunteer and philanthropy work.

In my late forties, I peeled off another layer of the onion. The last two years before we separated, I experienced a more meaningful shift in my mindset and approach to life because slowly, inch by inch, I began to focus on myself. My sons were older. I had more opportunity to slow down, stop being too busy, and take a hard look at myself. As I began to work more intentionally on myself, to evaluate where I was in life and where I wanted to be, I came to see that keeping busy was a crutch and a coping mechanism.

During this time, I was going to Al-Anon and seeing a counselor. Both interventions taught me to ask what I was doing to take care of myself, instead of hanging everything on the alcoholic in my life. Fixing my life wasn't—or shouldn't have been—about fixing Chad. I learned that I had a choice. Before, I felt like since I chose that life, since I chose to marry Chad, that meant I had to stay in it. That was my cross to bear, when really that belief was tied to my "good girl" upbringing.

I got to choose how I wanted to live. If I didn't want to live with the chaos of Chad, or the chaos of Joey after him, and feeling the need to change those men, then I didn't have to. I didn't have to keep banging my head against a wall trying to impose what I wanted for our relationships and how I thought our lives together should be. Once I freed myself from that type of thinking, I realized, *I don't have to live like this. I create my own life and happiness.*

One way to change is to replace the busyness and chaos with calm, quiet, and space. Once I stripped away all that noise, I was able to be who I am authentically and do what I want to do without being controlled or manipulated. Without the noise, I'm exponentially better at paying attention to how I really feel. My voice, identity, and intuition come through so much clearer now. As Dr. Clarissa Pinkola Estés explains:

The cure for both the naïve woman and the instinct-injured woman is the same: Practice listening to your intuition, your inner voice, ask questions, be curious, see what you see, hear what you hear, and then act upon what you know to be true. These intuitive powers were given to your soul at birth. They are covered over, perhaps by years and years of ashes and excrement. This is not the end of the world, for these can be washed away. With some chipping, and scraping, and practice, your perceptive powers can be brought back to their pristine state again.[5]

Meditation has been a huge part of my journey to find calm, quiet, and space. I started meditating around 2009, in large part influenced by yoga. When my kids were in middle school

---

[5] Pinkola Estés, *Women Who Run with the Wolves*, 74.

and slept in on Saturdays, I got up early and did yoga. My yoga teacher Carmen encouraged a daily practice. Because of her, I grew to love yoga and the restorative meditation at the end called Savasana, literally translated as "corpse pose." This resting pose helped me start to find stillness and listen to my inner voice, intuition, and the "voice" of spirit speaking to me.

For my forty-fifth birthday, my then husband's gift to me was a mindfulness course—or perhaps his assistant should take the credit. This is when I began to incorporate meditation into my life on a regular basis. During the course, we meditated for twenty minutes twice a day. Some believe meditation should be done a certain way, but there are many ways. I say whatever way enables you to cultivate stillness in this crazy world, do it. Whether you're sitting, lying down, or walking, whether you spend five minutes or an hour meditating, it all works. Today I try to meditate for thirty minutes every day. When I'm unable to, I notice that I'm not as calm or focused.

When I opened my business, Healing Soul Wellness & Fitness, I wanted to share the gift of meditation with others. It's one of the reasons I was drawn to sound healing, which uses the frequency and vibration of certain instruments—singing bowls, gongs, chimes, drums, and many more—to help with healing. I believe we are all energy, and life stresses can make our energy become stuck and stagnant. Sound healing is a meditation for the mind and body. It breaks up stuck energy, allowing the body to rest and heal.

Ideally, sound healing takes place lying down. I wear an eye mask to block out any visual distractions. Covering my eyes helps me stay focused on the sound and stay inside myself. When I go to sound healing consistently, I experience a huge shift in my nervous system. In an hour session I'm able to relax enough to lose time and sink into the sweet spot between sleep and wakefulness. I sleep better and feel better overall after I do sound healing. Many thanks to my sound healing teacher, Three Trees (yes, that's his real name), for teaching me sound healing so I can give this gift to others. While I've taken a break doing sound healing for others, I'm excited to be approaching a point in my life when I can return to it.

My Butterfly Guides

As I started to find my own voice, listen to my intuition, and come into my identity, butterflies came to have a very personal meaning and significance for me. The outer skin of a crawling, earthbound caterpillar hardens to form a protective casing called a chrysalis. Inside that chrysalis, the caterpillar undergoes a remarkable transformation known as metamorphosis. Caterpillars have to go through that transformation alone, without help from external forces. When they're ready, a fully formed adult butterfly, also known as the imago, bursts into the world. That butterfly is beautiful, resilient, and adaptable, and now has wings to fly.

Butterflies are transformation. They are growth. They are flight. Without the work the caterpillar has to do alone in its chrysalis, it can't become what it's meant to be. That struggle makes them stronger—and beautiful.

This positive symbolism and association with butterflies began for me when I met Pauline Olsen, my stepdad Harlan's mother. Pauline became an important person in my life.

My parents' mothers had both passed before I was old enough to know them, so Pauline became the only grandmother I had ever known. I met her when I was in college. She lived with her husband Fred in Sun City West, Arizona. Fred passed away in 1998 from Parkinson's disease, while Pauline lived many more years. She remained active for almost her entire life.

I was the first of my immediate family to move to Arizona, so I gravitated to Pauline. She always treated me and Heather like we were her grandchildren by blood. She was a great cook, and we enjoyed many dinners at her house. Pauline made dishes from scratch, which I always admired. Her home smelled like fresh-baked bread, ham, and desserts. My family spent most holidays with her, and I continued to do so after my divorce.

When she moved to Scottsdale to be closer to her youngest daughter Pam, Pauline and I developed an even closer friendship. In her final years, Pauline lost most of her sight, and she moved into an assisted living facility close to my house. I visited her often and took her to lunch. Whenever I read to her, she would usually fall asleep. She had a sweet disposition and was always giving away her chocolate candies. I still have one of her beautiful glass candy jars to remember her by. She lived to the age of ninety-nine, and I'm thankful for that.

Pauline had butterfly trinkets and knickknacks throughout her home and made us hand towels with butterflies on them, crocheting the top with a button so we could hang it over a stove or fridge handle.

The strength, beauty, and growth that butterflies represent helped me during one of the biggest periods of upheaval in my life. I separated from Chad in the summer of 2016, moving from the house we had built—where we raised our kids for nine years—to a house in Scottsdale. As he did every year, Chad left for Idaho in June to golf. I stayed in Arizona and, with the help of friends, packed and moved into my new house at the end of July. It was a stressful, sad, and emotionally difficult time. It was also a time of personal transformation.

As I drove around that summer, I kept seeing yellow butterflies everywhere, like they were guiding me into my new life, helping me grieve what had been lost, and encouraging me to spread my wings. They gave me courage. Their symbolism began to resonate with me even more, becoming a touchstone in my suddenly unfamiliar life.

That year I also received several gifts with butterflies on them. The first picture I bought for my new house was a large-framed mandala made of butterflies. The moment I saw it, I knew I had to have it in my new home to symbolize my transformation. Since then, I've acquired quite a few butterfly prints. I also own butterfly earrings, necklaces, and a butterfly sports bag. I even had a butterfly print at my wellness studio. It now hangs in my bedroom as a reminder of all that has been transformed in my life.

Whenever I visit Sedona, Arizona, my go-to spot is a restaurant called Mariposa. In Spanish, mariposa means "butterfly." The restaurant is decorated with beautiful wrought iron butterflies and has a stunning view of the red rocks of Sedona. A hiking trail called Adobe Jack passes through the hills right below the restaurant. I have great memories eating lunch on the beautiful patio, listening to their guitar player, and enjoying the sunny weather.

The powerful role that butterflies play in my life grew in 2023 when I didn't find the house I'm currently living in. It found me.

On a whim in September, I casually started to look online at houses for sale. I asked my real estate agent and friend Tim to send me some listings. I already had a few rental properties and loved looking at real estate. I wasn't planning to buy, but I thought, "There's no harm in looking!" I had remodeled the house where I currently lived, knowing I wanted to use it as a rental property at some point.

Tim sent me five listings, and one of them piqued my interest immediately. The next day, I arranged a viewing appointment. As soon as I walked through the front door of the house, I said, "Wow, I have a great feeling about this."

It immediately felt expansive, open, and full of light. It had an open kitchen to the family room, a large pantry, a tub in the master bath, and a low-maintenance yard with no grass. I could see all my furniture would fit perfectly inside. It checked all the boxes I wanted for my dream home.

The house had been on the market for quite a while. I told Tim, "Let's make a lowball offer and see what happens." I surprised myself because I've never been a spontaneous person. Usually I research a decision well, then think about it—sometimes to the point of analysis paralysis.

That night I woke up around one o'clock in the morning, and it suddenly hit me: The house was located on Mariposa Street. Sitting there in bed, I said out loud, "Oh my gosh, that's Butterfly Street!"

The moment I woke up, I also felt my dad's presence, like he was telling me to move forward. I was excited to realize Dad was with me and recognized this as a positive sign since he often visits me in my dreams. I had had a previous dream, for example, where I was sitting in an airport, looked over my shoulder, and saw my father.

"Oh! There you are, Dad," I said. He smiled and looked happy. Then I woke up.

In my dreams, my father is always smiling and happy. It makes me feel at peace.

Sitting there in bed, I knew what I had to do. I was supposed to move into that house. The offer was accepted, and the entire process went smoothly.

While the house on Mariposa Street was in escrow, I went to a conference in Florida. On the flight home, I sat beside a woman wearing an amazing outfit: head-to-toe butterflies on her shirt, scarf, purse, earrings, and phone. I nearly giggled out loud at the Universe seating her next to me. If I had any doubts about this house, they disappeared.

"I love all your butterflies," I told her.

"Oh, thank you," she said. "After my husband of twenty-five years passed away, I just started seeing butterflies everywhere." She showed me a blanket she'd brought with her on the plane that had his picture on it.

"I'm very sorry for your loss," I said. "What a great smile he had."

I told her about the house I'd made an offer on and how it was located on Mariposa Street. When we landed, I wished her well. She told me she thought all would be well with the butterfly house.

My decision to move into my new home on Mariposa Street came from my intuition. I had a feeling this was the right choice and something I had to do. I accepted it, and sure enough, the house has been perfect for me.

The Relief of Acceptance

Acceptance means to surrender to loving what *is* instead of what you think *should be* and sitting in the present moment. Mindfulness and acceptance keep us present without any conditions. So much of nonacceptance can send you into the regrets of the past and the anxiety of the future.

We want our lives to go a certain way. We like knowing. When we don't know, we are often fearful, and fear can keep us stuck and stunted. It's common in our consumer lives to think, *I need to have this to be happy. I need that in my life to be fulfilled. Getting a new job or having another child or finding a new partner will make me feel accomplished or successful. I just need that next new thing to fill the void.*

I have struggled to find acceptance throughout my life. Finally, I surrendered to the reality that I could not change my ex-husband and that it was not my job to do so. Accepting who is not compatible with you, and accepting that their energy doesn't work with yours, is essential to creating healthy relationships— and cutting out unhealthy relationships. I had to accept that we were meant to divorce each other and move forward in our lives separately, even if that meant changing the way our family would look.

When pursuing acceptance, we have to grieve first. We have to grieve our expectations. We have to grieve the loss of how we thought something would be, whether that's a relationship, a professional endeavor, a personal fitness journey, or the death of a loved one. When I lost my dad, the grief was humbling. Grief is a journey of ups and downs, and we have to accept that.

When we lose a loved one, we have to find acceptance that they are no longer a physical being on earth and in our lives. We are no longer able to pick up a phone and call them, meet them for dinner, or have a conversation about life. Instead of fighting against this painful reality, we have to accept that our relationship with them has changed. Our relationship now exists as remembrance, and their energy is no longer physically present— but it's still around us and within us. Our relationship is not over. It's changed.

Women have a unique need for acceptance. As women, we're all aging in a culture that doesn't want us to age—and doesn't appreciate or value our aging. But the real beauty of age is wisdom and experience. Acceptance means coming to terms with the inevitable, even when culture insists we keep denying it. Acceptance means not giving a fuck anymore about what society has pushed on us for our entire lives as women. It means accepting our bodies after we have birthed and breastfed babies and appreciating nature's gifts of life.

As a single woman, I've worked hard to accept, without limit or condition, that I am fully whole just as I am. I lack nothing. All those lessons, all the heartache and struggle, made me who I am. Acceptance imbues us with gratitude and relief. What a relief to finally know that I am enough.

Without acceptance, we can get lost in self-pity. It's a pity party—and intrusive, unhelpful, and harmful thoughts are the guests of honor. *Why me? This isn't fair. When is it my turn?*

It's easy to get lost in the deep dark hole of victimhood. I have hosted many pity parties, alone in my bed, crying myself to sleep, wanting things to be different, wanting the people I love to act differently. But searching for acceptance helped me understand that even though life is not how I imagined it would be, I could still sit with it, be in it actively, and find joy in it.

Acceptance gives us a choice. Either we accept the circumstances of our reality, or we don't. When we accept it, we become better able to grasp what to properly expect of and from our journeys, as well as the story we are capable of writing for ourselves. Fantasy stories are wonderful to read in books or watch on TV or in movies. But we can't live happily ever after by pretending we're in a fantasy. We can live happily one day at a time by actively using what "is" to make informed choices that help us grow.

PART 4

My Adoption Journey

CHAPTER 14

The Soul-Deep Effects of Adoption

I was the odd child out

When Adoption Heightens Difference

The impact my adoption had on me throughout my life took place on a conscious and subconscious level. Just knowing I had a birth mother who gave me away was a foundational truth about myself I couldn't escape. That truth created what felt like a hole in my identity.

As an adopted child, I didn't feel whole; I felt a void.

Because my adoptive parents also had a biological child—not to mention a daughter close in age to me—these differences between me and them felt more pronounced. Heather looked like our parents. She came from them; she was talkative and extroverted like my mom. She was artsy, creative, happy, and light. I was serious and quiet. I wanted to read and think deeply about things. After becoming an adult, my father often said, "Even as a child, you were three going on thirty."

The differences between me and my family felt profound for me, like I never quite fit in the family picture. None of them liked spicy foods, whereas I love them. In other families, I'm sure it's common for only one member to like spicy foods, or to have dark hair compared to the others' blond hair, or to have an introverted personality compared to the others' extroverted natures. What makes my experience unique as a child of adoption, however, is that these differences *felt more significant*. They weren't just a quirk of my personality. They were a genetic marker of how I was biologically different. They set me apart from my sister and my parents.

Somewhere in my subconscious, every difference, big or small, felt heightened and heightened my feelings of not belonging. These real and perceived differences also made me feel like being me wasn't okay. No matter how much they loved me (and they did), my parents and my sister couldn't keep me from believing, both subconsciously and consciously, that how I looked or how I did things was somehow wrong.

A majority of women go through phases in their lives when they struggle to accept how they look. The pressures, biases, and expectations from a fundamentally patriarchal society make us all hard on ourselves. For me, being adopted made my body image struggles seem even more pronounced and profound. The rest of my family all looked alike; I was the odd child out. This made it difficult to accept the dissimilarities between us. I had no one to identify with physically.

My parents assured me I was very wanted. They told me that adopting me was a loving act, not a bad thing. They told me how my mother couldn't keep me and how she wanted me to have a better life. That's why she put me up for adoption.

This is a common explanation when adoption is portrayed in movies, film, and other fiction: "She wanted you to have a better life." That may have been true, but being given away for whatever reason kept me from feeling like I belonged. And even though my adoptive parents chose to adopt me, since my biological mother had given me away, much of my life I struggled with an aching desire to be *chosen* by others, especially by men.

When Adoption Hinders Intuition

Being adopted and not knowing my true identity also made it more difficult for me to trust and listen to my intuition. I didn't have a fundamental trust in myself because I was always questioning my place in the world.

Who are my real parents? Who am I, really? Where do I really belong?

I don't remember when I found out that I was adopted. My parents told me at a young age, so it feels like I always knew. While this means I didn't have a traumatic "discovery" experience later, it also feels like the void inside me has existed since the moment my memory begins. That void has never *not* impacted my sense of identity and my development as a person. I suspect that even if I'd never learned I was adopted, that void would still exist inside me. I would still feel, intuitively, that I didn't quite belong.

From what they'd learned through the adoption attorney, my parents told me my biological father was Italian, and my biological mother was Italian and Irish. My mother had brown hair, like me. She gave me up for valid reasons. While I clung to these facts, they also had me create a fantasy to make sense of why they gave me up and to justify why they would give me away: *They were young and in love but couldn't afford to take care of me. They wanted me to have a better life.* Those few details weren't enough to satisfy me, though, and the love of my adoptive parents did *not* conquer all. This missing part of myself felt distracting. Endlessly questioning, wanting, searching—within myself or outside myself—took a huge amount of emotional energy. It fed the void and got in the way of me living the life I could have been living.

Why am I even here? What's my purpose?

If we don't know our own places in the world, we have a hard time building the confidence and self-assurance we need to exist, live joyfully, and move through life in a way that serves and uplifts us. Many of us find our identity and purpose in our family belonging, in our community, in our service to our loved ones. Identity and purpose are tied together. If we don't feel like we belong, there's always a degree of separation or disconnect between who we are—including our need to belong—and our purpose for being.

Why am I so different from my sister? Am I ever going to get any answers to these questions?

As an adult, I now know that biologically related siblings can be completely different in personality and physical appearance. That's the DNA lottery. Growing up, I didn't know that. All I knew was that my sister Heather and I looked and acted different, and she was connected to our parents in a way I was not. She had more of a right to be in our family than I did, so what business did I have being there? What business did I have *being* at all? Heather had an anchor that helped her belong, giving her an intuitive sense of who she was. All I had was a void inside me.

Westin and Wyatt also have very different personalities from one another, but they have never been driven to ask these types of identity questions—because they've always had an innate sense of identity and belonging within our family. They had that anchor, and I'm grateful for it every day.

Growing up in a family where we didn't discuss tough topics heightened my sense of being on my own as well. I had an intuitive sense that something was wrong in our household, but I didn't know my dad was an alcoholic, and my mom was struggling with everything that comes with living with an alcoholic. It's hardly surprising that a little girl would think the problem, the sense of wrongness, was coming from her, not from her parents.

As a kid, I wasn't given permission to do things my way or to follow my own intuition. When I was in high school, I wrote a letter to my dad asking where he was all the time and why he wasn't present in our family's life. I didn't understand the dynamics between my parents or that alcoholism was the root of the problem. When Mom told me not to give the letter to Dad, I felt confused and hurt. No one in our family acknowledged that Dad had a problem. Now I knew for sure that I shouldn't ask questions. Meanwhile, Mom kept herself incredibly busy—and tried to keep us busy and on task doing homework and extracurriculars—so she didn't have to think about any of it. My letter threatened that coping mechanism for her.

Her response also made me feel dismissed and shut me down. I couldn't express what I really wanted because I felt wrong for wanting to talk about why Dad was absent. My mom's reaction confused and upset me, eroding my ability to trust myself. Living with constant, low-level distress throughout our formative years—never feeling fully safe in our environment—prevents our intuition from developing the way it needs to in order to serve us.

Even knowing my parents loved me, I couldn't rely on their emotional support. The *not knowing* that was happening in my adoptive family was reminiscent of *not knowing* where and who I came from. It felt like none of the adults in my life could or would help me find the answers. I had to figure out all my identity questions on my own.

So that's what I did.

CHAPTER 15

The Influence of Adoption on My Career

I couldn't fill the holes in my medical history

S*tore Bought Baby* is a story about what a person goes through when they experience not knowing their biological family. It's about going through life with a void inside you that you desperately want to fill, even if only subconsciously, yet you may not know or remember what it feels like to *not* have it. That void becomes part of your identity. It affects how you see the world and the choices you make as you move through it. One of the ways I tried to deal with the void inside me was through my career choices.

When I was three years old, I came down with pneumonia and spent time in the hospital. Blood tests indicated possible leukemia, which prompted further testing. My hospital room felt cold and big. All the hospital rooms in this part of the unit were arranged around a dual-purpose waiting area for visitors and play area for kids. I don't remember my sister Heather visiting, although she most likely did, but for some reason I do remember Pete, my dad's friend from the Air Force, visiting with my parents. It's funny which memories stick with us and which don't.

The traumatic part of my hospital stay came when the medical team needed to perform a bone marrow biopsy on me. Bone marrow is a spongy tissue found inside certain bones. It is responsible for producing blood cells, including red blood cells, white blood cells, and platelets. Bone marrow samples are extracted so they can be tested for various medical conditions, such as blood disorders and infections. Because my white blood cell count was elevated, the medical team worried that I had leukemia, a cancer of the blood and bone marrow.

Two nurses took me into a sterile room with a cold, hard examination table and helped me lie down on my stomach. I was wearing a child-size hospital gown. With procedures like this (another example is lumbar punctures), the medical staff may prefer parents aren't in the room because it can be tough to watch their child go through it. They made the right choice in my case.

Immediately, I was upset lying down. My three-year-old brain got scared and confused. The nurses talked to me, trying to comfort me and keep me calm, but that didn't help. I looked over my shoulder and saw the doctor. Her dark hair was tied back in a tight bun, and she wore eyeglasses and a white lab coat. She was holding a *very* long needle.

The moment I saw that needle, I went ballistic. I yelled and cried, and a big snot bubble came out of my nose. Even as a three-year-old, that snot bubble filled me with embarrassment on top of being scared out of my mind. The nurses held me down to keep me from hurting myself or them. They had to get that bone marrow sample somehow. They couldn't just decide not to do the biopsy tests and hope I got better by myself. If it was leukemia, that's not something you recover from on your own.

The doctor made quick work of inserting the specialized—*huge!*—needle into the back of my hip bone to get the sample. It was over fairly fast. As a child, it *hurt*. As an adult, I'd probably describe it more as intense pressure and discomfort.

It took a couple days to get the results of the biopsy. My parents were beside themselves with worry, although I don't remember it.

I didn't have leukemia.

I *did* have thalassemia minor.

Thalassemia is a group of blood disorders that affect the body's ability to produce hemoglobin, a protein found in red blood cells that carries oxygen to the body's tissues. Hemoglobin consists of two protein chains: alpha and beta. Thalassemia occurs when there's a mutation or defect in one of these chains, leading to an abnormal production of hemoglobin. People of African, Asian, or Mediterranean (e.g., Greek, Italian) descent are more predisposed to have thalassemia. It's an inherited condition.

Thankfully, I had a less severe type of thalassemia that's not life-threatening if it's properly treated and managed. Basically, my red blood cells look a bit different from yours (unless you also have thalassemia). If I get sick, my symptoms may be more severe because my red blood cells have to work harder to do their job. This means I had to become more aware of my body and focus on taking care of it pretty early on in my life. Every year I get a complete blood count (CBC) test to check the quantity and quality of my blood cells, including red blood cells (hemoglobin and hematocrit levels), white blood cells (to assess immune function), and platelets (important for blood-clotting).

As I got older, I came to better understand that thalassemia is passed down genetically from biological parents to their children. This also made me realize that I didn't know any of my personal medical history because I was adopted. Every time I had an appointment with a healthcare provider for the first time, such as going to a new doctor or dentist, I had to sit in the waiting room struggling to complete a questionnaire about my medical history, for which I had too few answers.

I don't know.

I don't know.

I was adopted!

I WAS ADOPTED!

That's what I always wrote across the forms. My frustration grew deeper and deeper over time. Did my birth mother have thalassemia? What about my birth father? Or were they "thalassemia carriers," where someone has the mutated gene but doesn't experience any symptoms? I couldn't turn to my adoptive parents; they didn't have the answers. It was strange living with that blankness, that unknown part of myself that could have such a big impact on my life. It could literally mean the difference between life and death. Was there a ticking time bomb inside my body that I should know about—and that most children would know about because their birth parents hadn't given them away? The contrast with my adoptive sister Heather, who could answer those questionnaires and *did* know her medical history, exacerbated all my emotions about not being able to connect these dots.

To deal with the thalassemia and not knowing my medical history, I decided the best way to take control of my health—and, most importantly, to stay healthy—was to learn as much as possible. On top of that, I always had a natural curiosity about the human body and how it worked, so I didn't think of it as a chore.

My adoptive dad owned many nonfiction, educational books because he was always interested in learning new things. He enjoyed reading about all sorts of topics: languages, art, quantum physics, and psychology. He was a lifelong learner. His mother (my adoptive grandmother) wasn't able to get a formal education, so he grew up in a household watching her struggle to provide for her three kids after his own father (my adoptive grandfather) left them. This instilled in him a deep belief in the need for education and learning, and the environment he created for me and Heather fostered my natural curiosity. I owe my love of books and learning to my dad. I still have his *Gray's Anatomy* and *Taber's Cyclopedic Medical Dictionary* from my childhood, as well as many books he left when he died. I also loved a television show called *Quincy, M.E.* about a forensic pathologist who investigates suspicious deaths. That show increased my interest in human anatomy, and I'd daydream about what it would be like to be a forensic pathologist. Yes, I was a bit nerdy as a kid.

My commitment to learning as much as I could and taking care of my body remained fairly healthy. In other words, it didn't turn into an unhealthy obsession for me, and it didn't lead to unhealthy behaviors. In large part, this is because my parents didn't treat my disorder as something that, as a family, we needed to be fearful of or change our whole lives to accommodate. They had normal concerns, as any parents would, but they didn't pathologize me or my life. My thalassemia wasn't talked about unnecessarily, and they didn't stop me from certain regular childhood activities because of it.

One important element of this health consciousness for me was participating in athletics. I was always doing a sports activity of some sort. Softball and gymnastics were really big for me. I gained a love of gymnastics after watching Nadia Comăneci in the 1976 Olympics. I was in awe of her like so many other little girls and started gymnastics at the YMCA. I remember doing cartwheels everywhere I could: in the living room, in my yard, and at recess in school. Flipping and rolling around made me happy, and I wanted to learn more.

In junior high I was on the gymnastics team all three years. My favorite events were the balance beam and floor exercise. Surprisingly I can remember the compulsory routine on floor exercise I did all those years ago. In high school, I competed all three years. For my junior and senior years, we had German teacher Gunter Bohrman as our gymnastics coach. He was a former gymnast from Germany and pretty tough on us. Looking back, I appreciate his high expectations and drive. We had a bunch of club gymnasts on our team who were very talented. I was an average gymnast but still part of the depth of our team. Our team won the state title my junior year and placed second my senior year. I have fond memories with my teammates and made lifelong friends, many of whom I still keep in touch with. Being a gymnast taught me discipline and perseverance. The discipline helped me in many areas of my life and is probably how I got through nursing school while juggling two jobs.

I had many injuries over the years, as most gymnasts do, including stress fractures, multiple ankle sprains, and I even broke my nose falling off the balance beam. My hands always had multiple rips—open blisters from the parallel bars. I used to dry them out with a steeped tea bag, causing my hands to be tea-stained. It took two years after I was done competing for my right ankle to quit aching. Injuries, aches, and pains are part of any athlete's journey, but I wouldn't trade it for all gymnastics taught me.

Recently I was talking to a friend whose daughter was a gymnast, and we were commenting on how hard it is on the body, but how you learn to push through the pain. It was also mentally hard at times pushing through pain and setting aside any personal issues to perform. It hit me that I applied this to relationships also. No matter how difficult the relationship I was in, or how badly I was in pain mentally, I thought I had to persevere and see it through. I learned to never quit. It's like I was trained to suffer though toxic relationships and not give up on them. This awareness has given me a little more self-compassion. It is something I'm working on.

As I write this, I'm watching the 2024 Summer Olympics. Of course, gymnastics is always my favorite sport to watch. I am amazed by the athleticism and daring moves the gymnasts are doing today. I'm also proud that there is more attention and awareness being paid to the athletes' mental health. I applaud Simone Biles, the USA gold-winning gymnast, for stepping back from the 2020 Summer Olympics, listening to herself, and knowing she wasn't able to compete. She has brought attention to caring for one's mental health. Fortunately, sports have come a long way since I was an athlete in considering mental health and how a "coach for your mind" (a talented therapist) can help immensely.

In high school students are often given tests meant to tell them what professions they might be well-matched. My test results always told me to go into social work or nursing. I didn't have any interest in either of these career paths at that time. I briefly thought I might want to go into political science. Overall, I didn't have a clear career path yet.

When I went away to Western Washington University for my first year of college, I did fine, but I didn't know what I wanted to do. I couldn't help thinking, *Why am I wasting my parents' money here?* I moved back home to Kent, Washington, and transferred to community college where I could get the standard prerequisite classes out of the way for a less expensive price tag. A friend of our family was a manager at a plastic surgeon's office and got me a job there filing. While working in that environment, I befriended some of the nurses and watched some surgeries because a surgical center was right in the office. I thought surgery was very interesting.

Around the same time, I also began volunteering in a pathology lab at a hospital across the street from the surgeon's office. My childhood daydreams about what it would be like to be Dr. Quincy, the forensic pathologist from *Quincy, M.E.* came roaring back. I learned a lot about pathology and anatomy. Sometimes the lab would receive test orders and blood samples directly from surgery taking place in the hospital. I'd prepare the slides, and the pathologist would look at them right there. I also got to see some autopsies, which was eye-opening.

Getting this work and volunteer experience prompted me to think, *You know what? Maybe I should go to nursing school.* Those silly career tests from high school came back to me. I didn't dismiss the possibility of going into nursing just to satisfy my inner high school rebel. What I never considered pursuing was forensic pathology. I didn't have the self-esteem or the capacity to think outside traditional gender roles and tell myself, *Oh, as a woman, I could absolutely do this and still have a family if I wanted to.* In the back of my mind, all I knew to tell myself was, *Well yeah, I could be a nurse and still have a family. Lots of, if not most, female nurses do it.* I didn't have a female role model or mentor, either in the field of pathology or another medical field that would require longer schooling, who could tell or show me that it was entirely possible to be both a forensic pathologist and a mother.

After two years of community college, I applied to the University of Washington (UW) and got in. I transferred before applying to do a bachelor of science in nursing (BSN) at UW's School of Nursing. In the meantime, I took more random classes like statistics and calculus and only confirmed that I hated them. When applying to nursing school, the reference letters I got from the medical staff at the plastic surgeon's office and pathology lab were a big help. In hindsight, I can see the path I was on and the influence my adoption (the lack of my own medical history) played on my career. At the time, however, all these different steps were not intentionally or consciously informed by that aspect of my identity and life experience.

Nursing school was difficult, both the content that students have to learn and the logistics of getting to campus or the hospital where clinical rotations took place by bus or bike. When you're that new to learning something or navigating an unfamiliar environment, it's easy to feel like an imposter. So much about figuring out your career path is feeling like you don't know what you're doing. Medical professions also come with higher stakes because you have to keep patients alive and provide them care with dignity.

The first time I had to administer an injection to a patient, I worried often about not causing them pain. Inserting a needle into someone is an invasive act. The patient was already in a vulnerable state, having just come out of surgery. I didn't want to do anything to hurt them. That felt stressful and nerve-wracking. Of course, every time a nursing student does something new on a real person, they're doing it under the supervision of a registered nurse, so asking questions to receive proper help is important for the educational process. That first time administering a shot went perfectly fine. The nurse supervising me gave a little shrug and said, "Yup, that's how you do it."

While in school, I got a job as a nursing technician at a hospital in downtown Seattle. I worked on an oncology floor and also did extra work in labor and delivery. I have always been drawn to birth and the end of life. I've cried at the privilege of getting to see new life come into the world and of life leaving this world. It's a profound gift to witness the bookends of the circle of life.

I graduated in June of 1993 at the age of twenty-three. That summer, I took my licensing exam to become a registered nurse in Washington state before everything was computerized. The proctored exam was paper and pencil, and they escorted us to the restroom so there was no cheating.

After my adoptive parents divorced, my mom was very lucky to find her new partner Harlan. They married in March of 1991. I was very lucky too because Harlan's family is incredible. His kids Bret and Amber, as well as their spouses and kids, have been part of my life for more than thirty years. We've celebrated weddings, holidays, and birthdays together. I treasure these times and know my life has been fuller because of all of them. As part of that new extended family, I also gained an aunt, Pam, who became both friend and role model. She was in nursing school herself.

The summer I graduated, I visited Aunt Pam, Harlan's sister, in Arizona. I loved the sunshine and warmth, even in the hottest heat of summer. Because many people retire in Arizona, I could see there would be plenty of jobs in healthcare. There were also few opportunities for work in Washington, and those available didn't appeal to me.

I decided to move to Arizona. It felt like the right timing, and I was excited—especially when Aunt Pam invited me to come live with her. Back in Washington, I packed up a U-Haul, hitched my car to the back of it, and my dad moved me to Arizona. During the drive, I found out he was terrible with directions and that he loved the Red Hot Chili Peppers. It's a trip I will always treasure. The results of my licensing exam took six to eight weeks to arrive by mail at my mom's house in Washington. After opening the letter, Mom called me in Arizona and told me I had passed! I was elated.

I lived with Aunt Pam for six months. I love her dearly. Nursing licensing in Washington and Arizona have reciprocity, so I didn't have to take a new exam. Within three weeks of moving to Arizona, I got a job in the medical-surgical unit at a hospital in Downtown Phoenix. At the time, the area was known for its prostitution and drug deals. The unit treated anything and everything you can imagine, including gunshot wounds, illness from drug addiction, and a range of medical conditions.

While the job was a great learning experience, I didn't enjoy it. The stress was very real and very pervasive. The ratio of patients to nurses was terrible, and it was in such a rough neighborhood that sometimes staff weren't allowed to leave because gunshots were being heard nearby. Taking care of gunshot victims as a brand-new nurse is not a cakewalk. I'd also get patients with drug addictions telling me which of their veins would and wouldn't be able to take an IV line.

The high-pace, high-stakes environment affected the entire nursing staff and cultivated burnout and negativity for everyone. After a year and a half of being miserable, Chad suggested I look for a different job. Subconsciously, I'd believed that I needed to stick it out because it was my first job as a nurse, when really there was no reason not to look elsewhere. Like in my romantic relationships, I felt I needed to stay in a situation where I wasn't happy or fulfilled.

A friend of mine worked in home healthcare for a local hospital and connected me with a job opportunity. I interviewed, got hired, and loved that job. The pace was more civilized, patients were more comfortable in their own homes, and I looked forward to making home visits where I could talk with people one-on-one for longer periods. I loved the health teaching aspects of the job and the fact I got to drive around in the Arizona sunshine. In a hospital setting, there's always a time crunch to get in and out as fast as possible. Providing care to older patients was always deeply rewarding for me too. The job also gave me a fair amount of control over my schedule. Depending on my family needs, for example, I could work part-time, on weekends, or every other weekend.

This job worked well for me for several years, until Chad and I decided to have a second child. Quitting altogether was a difficult choice; I'd been raised—rightly, I think—to prioritize the need to make my own money and not rely on someone else's income. I had already been working part-time while taking care of Westin, who was a toddler. Chad was growing his real estate business, and I felt it would be less stressful for all of us to stay home full-time and raise our kids. I soon became pregnant with Wyatt after I quit working home health. Not having a paid job was mentally difficult.

While I dropped the weight easily after having my first son, it was much harder after my second. I joined a spin class to try to lose the baby weight. I enjoyed it.

One day, I suddenly thought, *Hey, I could teach this!*

That's when the seeds of my career journey into the fitness and wellness space were sown, although it would take me a couple more years to pursue a certification to teach spinning. Once I had it, I taught a handful of classes each week. That snowballed into an interest in becoming a personal trainer, so I took that on too. It took frequent studying, but I thought it was valuable for my kids to see me working toward an educational and professional goal. It reminded me of the environment of learning and curiosity that my dad had created for me as a kid. A few years later, I went on to get my certification through STOTT PILATES to teach Pilates as well. I was working as a personal trainer for a friend of mine, Seth, when I was introduced to Pilates. He was studying to be a Pilates instructor through Stott and needed to practice teaching the moves on someone. I was lucky enough to be that person. The first time I did Pilates, I was sold. It brought me back to my gymnastics days, and I instantly fell in love with it. Have you ever known that you were meant to pursue something? That it spoke to you so loudly that you were called to do it? That's how I felt about Pilates.

Pilates was created by Joseph Pilates, a German born in 1883 who was sickly as a child and turned to bodybuilding and gymnastics to help him become stronger. During World War I he used calisthenics to work with wounded patients to help them heal. He used springs from the bed mattresses for resistance, which is how the modern-day Pilates reformer got its start. He and his wife Clara opened their studio in New York in 1926. With his extensive knowledge of the human body, he helped dancers and performers rehabilitate, prevent injuries and better their craft. Pilates is centered around using breath with motion and using your core or "powerhouse."

It took me two years to get fully certified to teach Pilates. Stott has rigorous requirements to get certified, and only offered the classes locally every six months. They also require you to learn all the anatomy and physiology of the bones and muscles. My background as a nurse gave me an advantage with this aspect. I can't say enough positive things about Stott Pilates. The company is internationally known and highly respected. I'm proud to represent them.

Pilates made me a better trainer. I mixed Pilates with everything I taught, which included TRX and barre. It allowed me to be more creative with my workouts for my clients and myself. It taught me proper form and corrective exercises. Even after retiring, I can't help but notice when someone's posture or gait is off and can usually pinpoint the issue. I genuinely love Pilates and the positive results it can have helping a person's strength, flexibility, and balance. I do Pilates as a part of my cross-training exercise routine to this day.

At this time of my life, I began to shift into a holistic and naturopathic view of healing the body. While medications can help in emergency situations, supplements and alternative treatments can keep you healthy and your immune system elevated.

As a personal trainer, I went to clients' homes. Once I became a Pilates instructor, I created a make-do home studio and had clients come to me. Soon I realized I needed a larger, more professional space. Chad leased a large office for his real estate business. We decided I would convert the office's back area into a fitness space for both my own professional use and the employees' use. This is where I saw corporate and other private clients. I loved providing wellness and meditation teaching for the office. The location worked until Chad and I separated several years later.

Needing to get out of his office, I leased a new, bigger studio in Scottsdale and officially founded Healing Soul Wellness & Fitness, my own business. Opening a business allowed me to expand the services I could offer. In addition to personal training and Pilates, Healing Soul Wellness & Fitness grew to include yoga classes, sound healing, meditation (private and group sessions), and self-love classes (a one- to three-day group experience for women). I also took on business associates, including my sound healing teacher Three Trees, who led a certification program. I built a fantastic client base through referrals, word of mouth, and targeted marketing strategies.

Being a business owner was very fulfilling and very hard. I loved working one-on-one with people, especially older clients who needed help navigating their aging bodies outside a hospital setting or doctor's office. Helping them take care of themselves and stay as functional as possible, for as long as possible, gave me a sense of purpose and accomplishment. I was contributing in a way that aligned with both my professional skills and personal interests.

In 2023, I made the tough decision to close Healing Soul Wellness & Fitness. The business was at a stage where I needed to commit to growing it by bringing on new staff and other resources or close it when my studio's lease was up. My dad passed away at the beginning of 2023. The grief process prompted me to reflect and take stock of where I was in my life.

What do I really want to do with my time left on this earth? How do I want to spend it? After reflecting on these questions, I knew I needed to decrease my stress levels and spend more time with my mom, who was living at that time in an assisted living facility with moderate dementia. I also wanted to write about my experiences in life.

On to the next stage of my own growth and personal development, I decided.

This set me on the path to authoring this memoir and, through the writing process, realizing how intertwined my career path has been with my experience and identity as a child of adoption. I've always been curious about healthcare, with a drive to help others understand their bodies and take care of themselves. All that began with my own lack of knowledge about myself. Since I didn't know my genetic background, I was going to do everything I could to be healthy. I decided to gain as much knowledge about preventive medicine, fitness, health, nutrition, biohacking, and longevity so I could stay healthy and share my knowledge with others.

Even my initial interest in forensic pathology was connected to my lack of medical history. Many of the investigations that the fictional Dr. Quincy takes on are about filling in the missing pieces of someone's past: How did they die? What was their cause of death? Why do people keep secrets all over the place?

"I'm sick and tired of all this secrecy!" shouts Dr. Quincy.

He gets riled up and angry in almost every episode of the show. On some level, this resonated with me. Maybe if I'd been born male, I would have actually expressed my anger and frustration—hopefully in a healthy way—about not knowing my medical history and who my biological parents were. But traditional gender roles and the "good girl" trap I lived in meant I bottled up those types of emotions and fed them into the void inside me. Traditional gender roles also meant that I went into nursing, a more woman-friendly profession. It didn't occur to me that I could pursue forensic pathology, and I will always regret that.

Nevertheless, being a nurse and later digging into the field of fitness and wellness helped me build a foundation of medical literacy and understanding about myself. Focusing on my own knowledge gave me a certain amount of self-assurance, confidence, and self-awareness. Ultimately, I couldn't control if I'd ever fill in the holes about my past, no matter how much I tried to investigate and find my biological parents, but I could control how much I knew about my body and health in the present.

CHAPTER 16

Searching for My Origins

I'd been holding my breath for my entire life

The Long Search and Wait

It wasn't until I had kids of my own that I began trying to find my biological parents. I wanted to find them for myself, but also for my boys. Having kids lit a fire under me. Other than knowing I had Italian and Irish heritage, I didn't have any information about my medical history or birth parents' beliefs. That meant my boys didn't either.

When I was younger, I was told that to get more information, I'd have to travel to Florida where I was born and given up for adoption. Once there, I'd have to go to a courthouse and submit an appeal to have my adoption record opened. As a teenager and young woman, I never did this because the process seemed too daunting. By the time I even considered the possibility of looking for my biological parents, my family had moved from Florida to Washington state, so I would have had to travel from the West

Coast all the way to the East Coast. Then, as an adult with a family and kids to take care of in Arizona, I didn't have the time, the means, or the emotional support I needed to get to Florida.

In 2004, at the age of thirty-five, I hired a private investigator to look for my biological parents. Jenny helped me get as much information as I could, even if I didn't get all the answers. She also submitted a request on my behalf to the Florida Department of Children and Families for non-identifying information about my birth parents from the closed adoption record. Florida adoption law allows for the release of this type of information to "adult adopted persons." It does not allow for the release of identifying information.

The response letter to the request confirmed my place and date of birth, and that my "natural mother" was born in the fall of 1950. A few months after my birth, she was scheduled to attend an interview with Family Services. She didn't keep that appointment or call to reschedule. From what I can tell, she never had any more contact with Family Services. A week after the missed appointment, my mother's sister called Family Services and provided a range of information about my mother and the pregnancy. It's likely Family Services called my aunt's house to follow up about the missed appointment, which led to my aunt providing the information.

My mother was described as five feet, four inches tall and 118 pounds—which sounded similar to my physical description when I was the same age. She had brown hair, brown eyes, and a fair complexion. She was of Italian and Irish descent, Catholic, and a high school graduate. During the pregnancy, my mother was unmarried and lived with her sister until a short time following my birth. Soon after, she returned to a state in the northeast to take a beauty course.

"Because your natural mother was unmarried," I read in the response letter, "she could not care for you, nor did she want you." While pregnant, my mother was interviewed by Family Services, during which she stated that "placement was the best possible plan for [me]."

The letter reported I was the second child my mother had by my "natural father," who was twenty-two years old. He was five feet, six inches tall, with black hair, blue eyes, and a dark complexion. He was of Italian descent, Catholic, a high school graduate, and employed as a plumber. He played the drums in a combo.

My biological father told my mother that he would divorce his wife and marry her, but he never did. After she figured out that he wasn't going to keep his promise, the letter said she "had little desire for [me]." My older sibling was born in the fall of 1968, a year before my birth, and also placed for adoption. It was my aunt's opinion that my mother became pregnant the second time with me in an attempt to force my father to divorce his wife and marry her. "When this did not work out, she had no desire whatsoever to keep [me]."

The day after I was born, my mother signed the consent for adoption. The adoption was finalized on June 5, 1970.

Reading the callous details of that letter felt like a slap in the face. I was crushed. I'd had a fantasy in my mind that when the woman who gave birth to me put me up for adoption, she was young, in love, and making an intentional choice that was in my best interests. I pictured her and my dad together in college. After accidentally getting pregnant, they made the difficult decision as a couple to give me to a family because they were too young to care for me while they went off to conquer the world. Clearly, that was not what happened. The letter made it seem like I was a pawn in their toxic relationship, and my best interests weren't the most significant factor in the decision-making process. What a bunch of small-town drama!

Maybe it was true that my mother "could not care" for me and "had no desire whatsoever" for me, but none of that needed to be said or reported. I'm surprised they even put such cruel information in the letter. The response from the Florida Department of Children and Families included the phone number of Terri, the employee who was responsible for fulfilling my request.

I decided to call Terri to thank her for the information she had provided me and ask how I could find out more information through the court system. Right before we ended the call, there was a pause. I had an innate feeling that was overwhelming.

A little voice in my head said, *You need to ask her before you get off the phone.*

"I don't know why I feel this way," I said, "but was my birth mother's name either Debbie or Nancy?"

"The first one," Terri replied.

I was stunned, elated, and shocked all at the same time! The names "Debbie" and "Nancy" had just come to me. It was a divine moment of knowing.

"I can't share any identifying information with you," Terri clarified, "but I can answer 'yes' or 'no' to questions."

I was so excited. I knew from the letter that my mother's birth date was in the fall, so I started guessing months. "I think my biological mother's birthday was in September."

"No," Terri answered.

"October then."

"Yes."

Then I started on the specific day of the month. "Is her birthday between the first and tenth of October?"

"No."

"Between the eleventh and twentieth?"

I also guessed every letter of my mother's last name, which luckily wasn't too long.

That's how I was finally able to discover my biological mother's name and birth date. I was happy to learn that much. Thank goodness I kept talking to Terri because I almost didn't ask her any questions. I was flabbergasted. Intuitively, I somehow knew my birth mother's name. It was trapped somewhere deep inside me. I have no explanation for my good fortune. To me, it speaks to the child-mother connection in utero. After my delivery, I believe I was taken from her immediately. I don't think she held me, yet I somehow knew her name at that moment on the phone with Terri. I guessed her name by tuning into my intuition and acting based on what I was "hearing" in my own head.

After receiving the response letter from the Florida Department of Children and Families, the search hit a dead end—for the next ten years. Publicly available DNA testing and genealogy websites hadn't gained popularity yet. When they did, their existence gave me new hope. In 2014, I signed up for 23andMe and submitted a DNA test. During the wait for the initial results, I got really excited. It felt like I was on the edge of finding out something important.

When the 23andMe results didn't match me genetically with anyone, I was frustrated and disappointed. But I reminded myself that at some point in time, I trusted the Universe to decide when I was supposed to find out. Only then would somebody from my biological family do a DNA test and be a match. I also realized that not everyone would want to use or be able to afford these genealogy websites.

In 2019, I figured there was no harm in signing up for AncestryDNA too. Some people might use one service and not the other. As soon as I got my test results and figured out how the website worked, I sent out a few messages to potential matches. No one ever replied. While disappointed, I accepted the way it was.

However, I noticed slight discrepancies in the genetic breakdown of my ethnic makeup on the two services. A couple of the ethnicity percentage points were different between the 23andMe and AncestryDNA results. That was interesting and offered slightly different information. I wanted to put everything out there that I possibly could to maximize my chances of finding a connection—someday. Despite the silence and lack of matches, some hope stayed with me.

I don't know when this is going to happen, I thought to myself. *It may never happen. But there's still a chance.*

I wasn't resigned or cynical. I knew then, and even more so now, that the Universe guides us, and we have to trust in it. Over time, I experienced an acceptance that helped me come to terms with the void inside me and the strong possibility that I might never find out any more about my biological parents. As I discussed in Chapter 13, acceptance means coming to terms with how things are in our lives that we can't change (whether it's people, events and circumstances, or decisions we've made in the past) rather than constantly wishing they were different. Acceptance isn't passive. It's not about being a doormat and letting life walk all over us. It's about actively accepting the reality of our lives so we can make informed choices that help us grow. I surrendered it to the Universe. My spiritual path taught me to allow and trust in divine timing.

It Finally Happens

In mid-March 2021, I had a conversation with Joey's sister Sarah about all my efforts to find my biological family. Sarah and I had a unique connection because she had given birth to a baby boy at the young age of sixteen and decided to give him up for adoption. Unlike my failure to find my biological parents, Sarah had met her biological son years later when he grew up and located her. We were able to share with each other these different life perspectives, as a birth mother and as a child of adoption, and I valued that immensely.

"I've let it go," I told her finally. "It'll happen when the Universe wants it to happen."

Two weeks later, it happened.

Have you ever received an email, phone call, or text message that makes your heart race? Maybe your eyes widen, or you blink rapidly, or your breath stutters? The reaction is instantaneous, completely out of your control; your brain takes a few moments to catch up and process what's happening. I felt excited and nervous, but also cautious, and I did what I could to contain my excitement that this could finally be the answers I'd been looking for. So many times in the past I thought I'd found information that would lead to answers only to be disappointed. I didn't want to get my hopes up too high again.

At the end of March 2021, I received a message from a genealogist named Jessica that came through AncestryDNA's messaging chat system on a sunny Arizona afternoon.

March 30, 2021, 3:27 p.m.
From Jessica via AncestryDNA message
Hello. My name is Jessica, and I'm a professional researcher who's helping Kim extend her family tree. You are one of her closest matches, so I was hoping to speak with you about your family history in an effort to find out how the two of you are related. Any assistance you could provide would be really helpful. Kindest, Jessica

---

Oh my gosh, what is this? I thought breathlessly, reading Jessica's first message again and again. *Who is this? Is this it?*

I messaged Jessica back but heard nothing for the rest of the afternoon. That silence took on a particularly jagged edge—frustrating, urgent, and even infuriating. I could be very close! This could be it. I just needed someone to *talk to me*.

When I still hadn't heard anything from Jessica by seven o'clock in the evening, I decided to take matters into my own hands. I messaged Kim directly through AncestryDNA.

March 30, 2021, 7:08 p.m.
From Laura to Kim via AncestryDNA message
Hello Kim. It says we may be close family based on our DNA. I was adopted at birth in 1969 in Florida, and I am looking for my family. Any help would be appreciated. Where are you from? Thanks, Laura

---

I felt my adrenaline pumping as I sent the message, but I tried to sound calm and keep my message short and sweet. I also reminded myself that this might be a false alarm.

After a restless night of sleep, I went to my studio early the next morning, tired but hopeful. I didn't have to wait long.

March 31, 2021, 7:50 a.m.
From Kim to Laura via AncestryDNA message
Wow. I too was adopted at birth in 1968 in Florida. Brevard County, Melbourne Beach to be exact. Through a private attorney. I was able to finagle some paperwork out of the hospital I was born at, and it said my mother's name was Debbie Connors. Her mother's name was Margot, and she

---

was from New York. I also have the non-identifying letter of info from the state that says both my parents were of Italian descent and other data. Through this [I] have not seen many Connors in my results, wonder if that was a made-up name . . . do you have any info you can share? I am so excited to talk to you and compare notes and try to narrow down "who we are" lol. I have a wonderful genealogist helping me research this. Hey, would you like to exchange pictures to see if we look alike?

When I read Kim's first message to me, it felt . . . surreal. Without a doubt, she was my sister. We were similar in age. We were both put up for adoption in Florida. She knew the name of the woman who gave birth to me, who brought me into this world. Maybe most gratifyingly, this stranger, this *sister*, was excited to learn more about me and our shared family. She wanted to know *me* and "who we are," just like I did.

All the silence suddenly broke! Something shifted in me. That nagging void I'd lived with for such a long time changed shape. I had finally found a sibling—a sister! With this new revelation, I felt like the Universe had given me a huge gift, and I knew I would be getting more information. I also felt bonded to Kim because we had the same adoption story—at least about the beginning of our lives.

Laura to Kim – Same day
Oh my gosh – I have the same story! You have to be my sister! I was born November of 1969. Given up for

adoption in Florida. My birth mother's name was Debbie Connors. Oh my gosh – I have been wondering about you since I started this journey. I will send you a picture!

Kim and I exchanged photos. Wasn't that a novel experience! When I looked at her, my eyes teared up. I'd gone my entire life unable to see myself physically reflected in the family closest to me. But Kim and I look related. Certainly not identical, but like family. Like we come from the same place. Like we *belong*. We're both brunettes. Kim's hair is slightly darker than mine. We both have blues eyes. Mine are more gray-blue, whereas hers are bright blue.

Kim and I were both at work, so, between clients, we sent more messages back and forth. My hands kept shaking. I felt exhilarated. Kim was very enthusiastic and high energy. It didn't take long for us to swap cell phone numbers. Kim asked me to share my AncestryDNA test results with Jessica so she could try to narrow down who our biological mother was, which I did happily.

The DNA test results made it clear, however, that Kim and I were only half sisters. We shared a biological mother but not a biological father. This contradicted the information that I had been provided by the Florida Department of Children and Families, which was really disappointing. For seventeen years I'd thought I had a full sibling somewhere out there. Finding out that wasn't true deflated my spirits. I began to wonder what else I'd been told that might not be true.

In the months that followed, Kim and I got to know each other better. We spoke on the phone and messaged back and forth regularly. Unfortunately, Kim had a hard upbringing, and I feel it's her story to tell. Today she lives in the Southeast, is single, and has two grown sons, like me. She loves dogs and works in dog rescue. That's how Kim and Jessica met. Kim dropped off a rescue dog she'd been fostering to Jessica and discovered she was a genealogist. Jessica offered to help try to track down Kim's biological parents. That was the Universe at work.

I learned that, like me, Kim loves spicy foods. While it seems minor, that similarity felt meaningful. These types of subtle threads of connection (or disconnection) are incredibly important to how we view our own identity and find our place in the world, no matter at what age we discover them.

In November 2021, Kim and I met for the first time in person. We met up over a long weekend in Melbourne, Florida, where we were both born. We felt it would be healing for us to meet where we'd each been born and adopted. Both our early lives had been in Florida too, before we moved away. This in-person meeting felt dreamlike. We were strangers and half-sisters at the same time, just getting to know each other.

On that trip, we discovered that as kids, we had lived only ten minutes from each other in Florida. We took some drive-by pictures of our houses and realized we'd attended the same elementary school for a year. We also discovered we each have an affinity for mermaids because we grew up near a town called Weeki Wachee, renowned for its mermaid shows. Both of us have mermaids in our guest bathrooms as an homage to our Florida roots.

On that short trip, we bought matching shirts and talked for hours about our lives, kids, marriages, divorces, and family. I was thrilled to get to know Kim and learn about her life. As I talked to the shuttle bus driver on my way back to the airport, he asked why I was in Florida. After telling him my story, he exclaimed, "It's like a Hallmark movie!"

Indeed, it is.

A month later, on December 22, 2021, I was at my studio about to begin my workday, waiting for my first client to arrive, when Jessica called me with big news. Since March, the void inside me had shrunk in big and small ways. I couldn't say it had gone altogether, though. The deepest part of the void would always take the shape of my biological mother. I wanted to find and know my biological father as well, but my yearning and need to know my mother surpassed everything else. I wanted to know what she looked like. What kind of person she became. Who was this woman that I'd belonged to at the beginning of my life? Why did she decide to give me up? Did she really have "no desire whatsoever" to keep me?

"We found your mother," Jessica said.

I sprang out of my chair.

"You found her?"

"Yes."

"You—you're sure? Debbie Connors?" I asked, nervously pacing back and forth in the studio.

She laughed. "Yes. Debbie Paulson, maiden name Connors. Your bio mom lives in New York. She's been married for over fifty years and has two children."

Wow, I thought, stunned.

I'd been searching for this information for so long.

Jessica quickly texted me photos of my biological mother, including one from when she was young, and a few more current photos with her family. Debbie is brunette like me. We're exactly the same height: five feet, four inches, like the letter from the Florida Department of Children and Families reported. I could see a bit of myself in her, through the nose and mouth. My sister Kim actually looks more like Debbie than I do.

This is cool.

It's a moving and human experience to be able to look at someone and say, "Wow, I recognize a little bit of myself in them." Many people take family resemblances for granted or don't realize how important those similarities are to their identity and sense of self. I'd never had that experience before, except with my two sons, although that's different because I'm the mother in those relationships.

Before Jessica hung up, she said, "I'm going to find your biological father by Christmas." She committed to helping me find my biological father separate from her work for Kim.

It turned out Jessica moved very fast. That same afternoon, I received another call. The area code showed from New York. Typically, I don't answer the phone if I don't know who's calling. But as I stood there in my studio staring at the unfamiliar phone number, somewhere deep inside I knew that I needed to answer it.

"Hello?" I answered.

"Hi," the caller began. "My name is Kym. I just spoke to a genealogist named Jessica."

My heart stopped. "Oh my gosh, you did?"

"Yes! I'm your cousin on your dad's side. My son Gary is on AncestryDNA, and Jessica linked us together."

Cousin Kym—yes, both she and my biological half-sister have the same name, but with different spellings. She was warm, nice, and excited to speak with me. I felt an instant bond with her. I wanted to hear about her life and family. I wanted to see photos of her kids. Her son Gary, I would soon learn, resembles my son Wyatt.

I would also learn that it was Steve, my first cousin, that I had sent a message to as a potential match back in 2019. Steve didn't reply because he would have had no knowledge of my adoption or how it related to his family members.

Of course, I wanted to know everything my new cousin Kym could share with me about my biological father (her uncle).

"Uncle Luca passed away in 2018."

My heart sank. I was too late. I had missed him by only three years. The sadness I felt overwhelmed me. At the same time, though, I felt excited and grateful this new relative had reached out to me with so much information. Kym was welcoming and seemed to want to get to know me too.

Kym sent me photos of my biological father, which was very kind and made me even more grateful. I thought, *If I can't meet him, at least I have his family to give me information*. It turned out that I looked more like him than my biological mother. He also had thalassemia, which I later found out from another cousin Deanne, who's also a nurse. A significant puzzle piece in my missing medical history finally got slotted into place.

Luca was one of five siblings; he had four older sisters. That meant there were many more cousins than Kym. My family tree suddenly got much larger.

I also learned that although Debbie or her sister thought Luca was married at the time I was conceived, he wasn't. All that drama about my "natural father" reported in the letter from the Florida Department of Children and Families was overblown and likely misrepresented. Who knows what the truth is?

Evidently, as I've learned new information about my biological family, sometimes it has contradicted what I thought was true. I've felt exasperated at times, but I kept reminding myself to stay open-minded, go with the flow, and keep digging as I kept trying to fit puzzle pieces together. I soon accepted that solving this family puzzle was part of the process of finding out about my family. I've discovered pieces that didn't fit initially and been led down many paths that I might not have expected.

But on December 22, 2021, the Universe wanted my lifelong search to end. Finally, The Universe decided, "The void inside you *can* be filled. You don't have to live with it forever." It felt like a big sigh of relief, like I'd been holding my breath my entire life, and suddenly I didn't have to hold it any longer. I knew that no matter what came after December 22, 2021, that day had given me some closure, and those two calls from Jessica and Kym became the best Christmas gifts I could have ever asked for.

CHAPTER 17

My Biological Mother's Family

I'm sorry she carried this alone

Finding the Truth, More Questions, and Peace

In 2021, I found out who my biological mother and father were. I also found and met my half-sister Kim, who had also been given up for adoption at birth. That year felt like a whirlwind of discovery. Many of my questions remained unanswered, though.

In January 2022, Kim and I sent Debbie a letter by certified mail to ensure she would get it. We told her that we'd met each other through AncestryDNA and knew she was our biological mother. We asked if she would be open to speaking, but we didn't want to pressure her or cause any discord. We included a couple photos of us that we'd taken when we met in person in November 2021.

It took a few weeks before we got a letter back from Debbie in February. Not surprisingly, she was overwhelmed. Debbie explained how, just before she found out she was pregnant with Kim, her own parents had been in a bad car accident. It was a terrible time for her family. Her father was killed, and her mother spent time in the ICU with a broken back and never fully recovered. The late 1960s were a different time for women. Birth control was not readily accessible, and being unmarried and pregnant was taboo, especially if you were Catholic.

Debbie only referred to one father, her boyfriend at the time—even though the results of the AncestryDNA test revealed that Kim and I are only half-sisters. Debbie said her boyfriend didn't want to get married or take care of a baby. She didn't mention him already being married, as the letter from the Florida Department of Families and Children had.

When she got pregnant, Debbie went to Florida to stay with her sister Maria, gave birth to Kim, put her up for adoption, then returned to New York. Even though her boyfriend had dumped her, they bumped into each other around town. He'd give her rides whenever he saw her, and she was still in love with him. They became a couple again, and she got pregnant with me.

Debbie went to Florida a second time and gave birth to me. Both adoptions were closed and completed through a private lawyer. She didn't include anything about her boyfriend's reaction to the second baby or how their relationship ended.

I'm sorry Debbie carried this alone all these years. I have compassion for her situation and only send her healing. That's a lot for a young woman to carry all these years.

It saddens me that women in our not-too-distant history were shamed when they became pregnant out of wedlock, then were frequently sent away until the child was born. If they were religious, they were often treated poorly and as "sinners." Some of these young women had their babies taken from them without their permission and sold to adoption. It seems unfair that the young men had little-to-no accountability for being half the cause of a pregnancy. I support a woman's right to control her own body and know what's best for her. It's dangerous when religion and politics get involved in what is a personal decision and often a medical procedure for a woman's health. It makes me sad that Debbie really did not have any other choice but to have two babies that she clearly was not ready for and did not want. I often think about what Debbie's life would have been like had she had easy access to birth control. At that time women needed permission from their parents or husband to access birth control. Abortion was not legal at this time, and many women took the chance and had "back-alley" abortions that were often not clean or safe. Many women died because of this. Thankfully Roe v. Wade was passed in 1973, but unfortunately the Supreme Court overturned it in 2022. I believe those against it are disconnected from the larger picture of a woman's right to bodily autonomy and that it is a medical necessity in many cases.

Debbie gave us some medical history and her phone number in her letter but said she couldn't have a relationship with us right now. She had put up a wall around that time in her life. In 1970, Debbie married a man and went on to have two more children, Amy and Brandon. She kept and raised her children in a northeastern state.

I sent Debbie a text message thanking her for her letter and letting her know that my mom Annette wanted to thank her for having me. Then I took some time to process everything I'd learned, everything I didn't know yet, and how I wanted to move forward. Figuring out what I wanted to do next—if anything—took deep reflection and consideration.

It's too bad my birth mother decided not to engage or interact with me, but she's on her own journey, and I have mine. Although her decision disappoints me, I will not be a victim or a martyr and wallow in something that's out of my control for the rest of my life. I will live the best life I can.

Feeling My Way Through New Relationships

As I meet biological family members of mine, I'm approaching my interactions and relationships with my newly discovered half siblings with caution. How I'm going about it shows that I've grown and gained agency, self-worth, and a voice for myself. I was the one to send Facebook messages to Amy and Brandon. In May 2022, I took the initiative to send my story to them, knowing I was opening myself up to potentially being hurt—yet believing I was strong enough to handle it. I did not want to wait another ten or twenty years to let them know about me and possibly miss out on some type of relationship with them. I had nothing to lose.

I explained to them who Kim and I were, what Debbie had told us about our adoptions, and that we wanted them to know we existed. I ended my message to them by writing, "We would love to speak to you if you are open to having a conversation. We don't want anything from you—just to know that you have two half-sisters. If you would like to call or text, here are our phone numbers."

Amy messaged me back, showing some curiosity about me. "That's a lot to take in," she wrote. "I would really like to connect and talk to you both. I'm floored. I think I'd like to take a little time before I reach out. Thanks for your openness and graceful way you handled it all. I'll reach out in a few weeks."

As we messaged back and forth, we exchanged photos and arranged to have a phone call a week later. It felt like a flurry of messages as we both reacted to our strong emotions about such a life-altering event.

Amy shared a bit of information that made me emotional. "I think you look a lot like Mom, and your profile is so interesting to me," she wrote. "Your career path is the interesting part. Mom's maternal side, the Bianchis, have a history of being healers, herbalists, in Italy. Our great-grandmother Gina came over when she was a little girl."

Wow.

Reading that was meaningful. It became a thread of identity and belonging I'd never had before. Many people take details like these for granted, but I'd been waiting my whole life to get them. It was both a gift and something I deserved to know. On both sides of my biological family tree, I had grandparents from Italy.

Everyone deserves to know where they come from.

On the day of our phone call, Amy messaged to say she had to cancel. She was overwhelmed and needed more time to process what she'd learned, and for other busy parts of her life to settle down.

"I just need to be in a less rushed place," she wrote. "I hope you understand. I'll reach out in a week or two."

I felt sad and disappointed, but I also empathized with Amy, understood where she was coming from, and accepted her choice. I knew this would be a lot for someone to process, especially learning she had not only one, but *two* half-sisters she hadn't known existed. I put myself in Amy's shoes and realized we might have scared her off. I felt okay backing off and seeing if anything might happen later. I called Kim and told her that Amy had canceled the call. Kim was quiet and probably felt disappointed too. She didn't say much.

It would be great if Amy and I could build some type of relationship over time, but I didn't hang all my hopes and dreams on it like I might have done when I was younger. If she wanted to get to know me and be part of my life—fantastic. If she didn't, I'd be okay with that. I knew it must be difficult for Amy to feel her way through this situation because she's very close to her mother. Interacting with me in any way meant going against her mom. I had no clue what that looked like between the two of them, and it must have been tough. Amy explained briefly that Debbie was completely shut down and full of shame about that part of her life.

At the end of June 2022, Amy messaged to say she hadn't forgotten about me. She described everything she had going on, including traveling for work and welcoming her first grandchild. I congratulated her on her new grandbaby and said I looked forward to connecting again when she was able. That was the last I heard from her for a long while.

During our initial exchange of messages, I learned a little about Amy. She's a culinary teacher who works in a high school while doing culinary entrepreneurial activities on the side. I was interested in asking her whether she enjoys spicy foods like me and Kim and some of these other preferences that may or may not indicate a shared genetic trait. I also think, like me, Amy has tons of empathy, and she's a big believer in the Universe giving us what we need when we need it.

In December 2023, I thought about reaching out again to wish Amy a Merry Christmas and Happy New Year. While deleting some old Messenger messages, I accidentally sent Amy a thumbs-up emoji. I'm glad for the accident, as she replied and said she'd been thinking about me.

"I looked back at our messages and realized how long it had been since we've made contact," Amy wrote. "I'm in a much different place than when you reached out; it was definitely a season of change for me at that time. How are you?"

We exchanged several messages on Christmas Eve—a lovely Christmas gift. I told her about my dad passing at the start of 2023, and how I was in a better place after a year of grieving and healing. We both shared how we'd moved closer to our moms to be able to help out more and provide care.

"I think about it from your point of view all the time, and yes, I would love to get to know you and stay in touch more consistently," Amy wrote. "Mom is still very much in pain with that time in her life and not willing to connect. I am sorry about that."

"I understand and I respect your mom's decision . . . I know what it's like to be protective of your mother."

Given the way Debbie felt about Luca rejecting her, it's little wonder I've always felt unworthy and unwanted and why I sought out love so much, even in harmful or toxic relationships. The trauma that women experience—the way we're treated, the social environment we live in, and the thoughts we have about ourselves—must have a huge impact on a fetus in utero. All that hurt, negativity, distress, confusion, and insecurity that my biological mother felt as a young woman . . . she felt all that while pregnant with me. I can only believe that I must have known the smell and the sound of her heart, having spent nine months in her womb. After all, how could I have possibly known her name was "Debbie" if there was no connection between mother and baby in utero?

Another author who has influenced my life is the work of psychologist Dr. Nicole LePera. In her book, *How to Be the Love You Seek,* she talks about body consciousness and how disconnection can occur in utero. She writes, "For me, I believe it started in utero, when I was immersed in the stressed physiology of my mom's dysregulated nervous system. If your mom didn't feel safe inside her body, you probably didn't feel safe inside her body when you were developing, either." She then adds that "research corroborates my experience, showing that elevated levels of the stress hormone cortisol in pregnant women can cause larger amygdala volume in the developing child, leading to a dysregulated stress response and anxious behaviors."[6]

My adopted mom told me I had colic as a baby. Babies with colic are often fussy, gassy, and don't sleep well. I can only wonder if my biological mother's mental state, along with me being taken away from her, contributed to this condition I had as a baby.

In February 2024, I reached out to Amy before Valentine's Day. I told her a bit about my holiday and how it was calmer this year, although also difficult as the one-year anniversary of my dad's passing came and went. She told me about her growing entrepreneurial work and high school teaching program, including a fundraising event with her students and a local golf course community that went well.

"I'm looking forward to getting to know you," Amy wrote. "I don't always know how to proceed with our relationship. It's been more of a reaction than proactive, just given the nature of it all. Do you prefer talking or texting? I appreciate that you've been leaving it in my court. I'm curious as to what you prefer?"

Amy was diplomatic and, I think, expressing that she wasn't feeling pressured as we navigate this together—because it's kind of an awkward thing for both of us. Imagine meeting a close blood relative for the first time as an adult and trying to get to know them while the mother who birthed both of you doesn't want to interact or participate. Talk about complicated!

In reply to Amy, I wrote, "It's completely up to you, although at some point in time, I would love to have a phone call with you. But again, that's completely up to you. We'll just see where it goes."

---

[6] Dr. Nicole LePera, *How to Be the Love You Seek: Break Cycles, Find Peace, and Heal Your Relationships* (Harper Wave, 2023), 129–30.

We ended up speaking on the phone in March 2024 for an hour and a half. At the beginning of the call, I told her honestly, "I'm nervous to talk with you. I don't know how this is going to go."

Amy laughed kindly. "Yeah, it's kind of like online dating where you message people and then finally talk in real life."

That broke the ice. She was funny and down to earth, and the call was easy conversation. We answered each other's questions and shared highlights about our lives. We both have adult children in the same age range, and we both went through divorces after long marriages. We also discussed some family medical history, including the heart issues that Debbie is experiencing. Amy was curious and open, and I'm grateful for that.

"What are your expectations for this?" Amy asked at one point.

"I don't really have any expectations," I replied. "I just want to get to know you as a person. We'll see where it goes." As I started to feel more comfortable in the conversation, I got more excited to learn more about her.

Amy explained in a bit more detail how the initial discovery about me and Kim went for her. When she saw my first message on Facebook, she told Debbie, "You need to stop posting on Facebook, or someone's hacked into your account or something. I got this message from these people saying they're your daughters and you gave them up for adoption."

Debbie could have gone along with Amy's idea about my message being some sort of scam, but she didn't. She could have denied who Kim and I were, but she didn't. Instead, she burst into tears. She had a trauma response.

The effects of trauma can be apparent in how people go about their lives. They may let chaos into their relationships. They may let in negativity or harmful behaviors. They may suppress emotions, experiences, and memories. Sometimes their guard can be up so high that they come off as defensive or unapproachable.

That is often coming from a need to protect themselves from getting hurt again. It doesn't take a trained psychologist to realize that hurt people hurt people—or push other people away before they can be hurt.

Once Debbie got through the initial shock, she shared with Amy that she had really loved my biological father. He had broken her heart; I do believe that. It also became clear from Amy's account that Debbie thought—and likely still thinks—that Kim and I have the same father. As a young woman, she might not have been educated about her menstrual cycle or how pregnancy works.

Do I tell her? I thought.

"You know, I have to be really honest and transparent with you," I said after hesitating. "I'm not going to hold any of these facts back. Kim and I don't have the same father."

"Oh," Amy said, surprised. "I can see why maybe Mom wouldn't tell the truth about that."

"Well, I don't know that she necessarily lied. She might not have known."

It's not implausible. Debbie was eighteen years old and no doubt didn't receive a decent reproduction education. It would also explain why the 2004 letter from the Florida Department of Families and Children reported that Kim and I had the same father, and why Debbie only referred to one father in her letter to me and Kim. Even if she'd had doubts, a large part of her may have wanted Luca to be the father of us both.

Amy also told me about her cousin Krista who lives in Florida. Krista's mom Maria, who died in 2021, also gave up a baby for adoption. Maria told Krista when she was nineteen years old, and Krista has now decided to look for that half sibling. Amy said we would get along well because Krista is a shaman and big into energy. She connected us, and we had a phone call.

During that call, I knew that Krista and I speak the same language. She has done a lot of healing and work on herself. She talked about my biological mother Debbie (her aunt). She told me that the man I'd thought was Debbie's father and my biological grandfather, Bruce Connors, who died in a car accident when she was eighteen years old, was actually Debbie's stepfather. Debbie's biological father Harold ran off with another woman and started a new family. Bruce ended up adopting Debbie and her two siblings when she married Debbie's mother Margot.

That news surprised me, to say the least. My biological mother, who gave me up for adoption, was herself a child of adoption. The circumstances were different; she wasn't put up for adoption as a newborn, her siblings stayed together, and her biological mom kept her. On the one hand, it felt like another missing piece of my puzzle, a part of my generational story. On the other hand, it felt like a new puzzle piece had been created because I'd gotten the identity of my biological grandfather completely wrong! My family story just kept getting more interesting.

Krista sent me photos of Harold, and I kind of see the resemblance.

The in-laws of my adoptive sister Heather do hobby genealogy work, so I introduced Krista to them. I also gave her Jessica's information, as she was able to help connect me with Kim. Krista is now on her way to finding her half sibling. Krista and I have spoken a few times, and we resonate with each other. We both have done loads of work to heal and speak the same spiritual language. I'm amazed at the power of connection and the people the Universe brings into our lives. When I set out on my journey to find my biological parents, I never thought much beyond them. It didn't occur to me that I'd be opening myself up to all these new connections: new extended family; new opportunities to build relationships; new possibilities for meaningful caring, consideration, and growth.

Every time I talk to someone new, I learn something I didn't know—or something I thought I knew turns out to be wrong. The void that I lived with for so long recedes a bit more with each new puzzle piece, but the pieces also bring surprises and the unexpected complexities of people's real lives. For most of my life, my only goal was to find my biological parents. After I found them, the answers still weren't straightforward because people and relationships are complex and messy.

I also gained a deeper understanding of what family should be. Family is who loves you. It should be as simple as that. Blood relations can be extremely meaningful and powerful, but they're not everything. When a child of adoption goes on a journey to learn who their biological parents are, they may find answers or people or truths that disappoint them. Through my own journey, I realized how lucky I've been to have had family around me all my life. First, I had my adoptive family. Later, when my adoptive mom got remarried, I also had my stepfamily. Then I had in-laws from my own marriage and my adoptive sister's family. I'm blessed to have had all these wonderful, loving people in my life.

Today I have a new biological family. I look forward to getting to know them better, as well as a new appreciation for the family that has been in my life for years.

CHAPTER 18

My Biological Father's Family

I'm grateful it's been so easy

My biological dad Luca had four older sisters: Mary, Frances, Sally, and Angie. Like Luca, Sally and Angie had already passed away by 2021 when I learned who they were. But all four sisters had kids of their own, which meant many cousins (nine total!) that I could potentially meet.

Cousin Kym, the first person I met on Luca's side of the family, quickly connected me with my cousin Deanne, who lives in South Carolina. We messaged back and forth, and I learned she was coming to a conference in Scottsdale in January 2022.

"Would you like to get lunch?" Deanne asked.

"Absolutely!" I wrote back.

We met at a restaurant called Flower Child and talked about our lives and the family.

When Deanne first saw me, she said, "Oh yeah, I see it in your eyes. You have the family eyes." That was cool to connect like that and for her to be able to see our shared family resemblance in me.

She also told me about my dad. Luca liked to laugh. He played in a band and was quite athletic. Luca and his siblings grew up extremely poor. Their own dad, my biological grandfather, also named Luca, immigrated to the United States from Sicily when he was seventeen years old. Luca (Sr.) married an American Italian woman named Louise. He died young, when Luca (Jr.) was only seven years old.

Getting to know Deanne as a person, separate from anything she could tell me about my dad, was equally wonderful. We talked about our respective work and careers. Deanne had been a nurse and, by 2022, had moved into medical sales. The shared nursing career between us was another point of connection that I valued.

Like me, Deanne has children, so we talked about them and motherhood. She's very nice, and our lunch was such a positive, easy meeting. I was grateful to have met Deanne in person. Her conference in Scottsdale felt like the Universe had given me a gift.

Megan and Steve are siblings and two more of my "new" cousins. Megan lives in Florida, and Steve lives in Georgia. Steve and I are only friends on Facebook; he has kids around the same age as mine, so we've sent each other a few messages about that. In 2022, Megan reached out to me more intentionally. Like Deanne, she's also nice. She even sent me some photos and gave me a bunch of information about the family.

I got on a FaceTime call with Megan and her husband, as well as her mother Shirley and Shirley's husband Bob. Shirley and Bob are my aunt (biologically) and uncle (by marriage). Shirley had dementia, so her memory wasn't what it used to be. Still, it felt lovely to meet her.

"Luca had the best laugh," Shirley said.

Megan nodded. "And he loved food and music."

I felt grateful to them for sharing those seemingly small details with me. I could finally know concrete things about Luca. How could I not think about how I took band in school and played flute for years? I have rhythm and have always loved anything musical.

I must have gotten that from my biological dad, I thought. *That's so cool.*

The emotion that came with discovering these similarities between us made me realize I *did* want to have inherited something from my dad. It was important to me. No matter how small, no matter that I learned about it secondhand from his family, it's still a tangible connection that's meaningful to me, especially because Debbie's reaction when we made contact was filled with negativity and trauma.

Learning about Luca felt pure.

During that FaceTime call, I told them, "I got a letter from the Florida Department of Children and Families that said my mom was trying to get pregnant with me so that my dad would leave his wife."

Megan, with input from the others, replied, "That's not right. Because Luca was very young. He was either in high school or right out of high school when he got married since his girlfriend was pregnant. But then she lost the baby, and they had the marriage annulled. He wouldn't have been married when you were conceived."

It's possible there was some overlap with Luca's short-lived marriage and Kim's conception, but even that seemed a bit far-fetched. I don't know what the truth is, and it doesn't really matter. He never had any more children. Maybe losing a baby to miscarriage when he was young scarred him, then on top of that deciding not to take care of the baby (or babies) when he and Debbie got pregnant—to his knowledge, either once or twice. (Remember, Kim and I know we don't have the same father, but Debbie and Luca may have never known.) Luca was only twenty-two years old when I was born, and Debbie was only twenty. They were both very young and had already gone through too much tragedy.

But Luca clearly lived a full life, and I'm happy for that. It gives me comfort for some reason. He enjoyed a relationship with a woman named Bonnie for forty-six years, though they never married. I was told they were deeply in love and may have been the type of soulmates who can't live without each other because Bonnie sadly committed suicide after Luca died. I wish I could have met them and learned more about their story directly from them.

Mary passed away in February 2023, just a month after my adoptive dad Glenn passed as well. Megan, Steve, and I sent condolences to each other. That's the majority of the contact I've had with my biological dad's family.

Soon after my cousin Kym and I first made contact in December 2021, she invited me to visit her in New York. It was such a busy time for me with my business that a trip wasn't feasible. In 2022, much of my emotional headspace was occupied with contacting my biological mom's side of the family and processing everything that came with that. Then, in 2023, I spent most of the year working through the grief of Dad's passing, healing my heartbreak, and reflecting on what I wanted to do in the next chapter of my life.

Now that I have more time and available headspace, I hope to get to know my biological family, visit them, and even maybe plan a family reunion on my father's side. Meeting more of them

in that type of setting, while possibly overwhelming, could also be incredibly thrilling—a chance of a lifetime.

For most of my life, I focused first and foremost on what it would be like to find my birth mother. To a large extent, the one-of-a-kind connection between mother and child in utero is immutable. It's foundational to the human condition and to human existence as a whole. The depth of that connection cannot be explained, yet most mothers can inherently understand it as something very real, even if the emotions and circumstances they attach to it differ dramatically. So finding the woman who had been my first connection in life was the most important part of my search.

I never considered how wonderful it would be to have members of Luca's family engage and embrace me without hesitation. There have been no uncertain or negative parts to my experience with them. They've been open, uncomplicated, and accepting. They've shared all this information with me that has also connected me with my Italian heritage in a way that I never had before.

Recently, I watched a biographical drama film called *Cabrini* about the life of Francesca Cabrini, an Italian Catholic missionary who lived from 1850 to 1917. She came to the United States to help other Italians, including Italian orphans who were flocking to the country, many in extreme poverty. She was an amazing woman. As I watched *Cabrini,* for the first time my heritage truly resonated with me and felt real. My Italian heritage suddenly became part of my identity, a source of pride and knowledge and connection to the beautiful parts of humanity. It touched me immensely because my grandparents on both sides immigrated from Italy and experienced poverty. I told my boys about the film, hoping it would also help connect them to their heritage.

Because I hadn't thought as much about my biological dad and his family throughout my life, I wasn't expecting the experience I had. Maybe because I had fewer expectations and hopes about Luca, the Universe saw fit to exceed them. Unexpectedly, I can relate more to some of Luca's traits. I look more like Luca's side of the family than Debbie's side. He was musical like me. He was athletic like me. He had thalassemia like me.

I'm sorry I never got to meet Luca. I feel in my heart he would have wanted to meet me. Maybe that's wishful thinking, but I do. That sadness will stay with me for the rest of my life, but it's not a bitter sadness. I'm grateful to have the connection to the rest of his family. I'm grateful it's been so easy.

After I discovered my biological father's identity, I looked Luca up online and found his obituary. It's unique, and whoever wrote it put personality into it. The author is unknown but believed to be a member of the New Earth Band, the last band Luca played in.

> Luca M. Gambino, 70, of ******, NY, passed away on Friday morning, March 30, ****. (Information from ****** Cremation Service.)
>
> Luca Gambino, Oct. 1, **** to March 30, ****. Do the math. He was 70. He died on Good Friday of organ failure.
>
> He was born on a cold October day in *******, NY. His father was Luca Gambino of Sicily. His mother was Luisa Ricci, American Italian. He grew up on River Street and was an excellent fisherman.
>
> Being Italian he got the real deal and was usually disappointed with Italian restaurants. He would go to a festival

and eat something, then come home and duplicate it. He created a lot of wonderful food from his small kitchen.

In high school he played several sports, was the co-captain of the football team, and was on the first lacrosse team at Eastern High School. He helped start a drum and bugle corp. at an early age, and music was always the major passion in his life. He was in several groups, the last being the New Earth Band.

Throughout his life he had many jobs, among them was a gas station attendant, a cable installer, an apprentice plumber, and a bartender. He did construction and painted houses and could fix pretty much anything.

He was the happiest, of course, with a drum in his hands. Bonnie was his loving companion of forty-six years. They grew up together.

He has four older sisters: Angie, Shirley, Mary, Frances, and half brother Todd.

He has ten nieces and nephews and several great nieces and nephews.

Luca was not your average bear, and his remembrance gathering will reflect that. It will be Sunday April 22 at 11:00 a.m. in Cascade Park. Put it in your request to the good weather gods for a dry, warm day.

Please make generous donations to your local hospice center. Every one of them was truly amazing in the compassion and skill they showed. We were very thankful for their loving support for the past four months.

Above information from the family.

An obituary was published in *The Crown Leader********, NY, on April 10, 2***.

Closing

I'm just getting started

Discovering all the unexpected information about my bio-logical family members while also growing more into myself has helped me find my own identity, my own person, and my own voice. I now know that I'm not only a store bought baby. I'm as homegrown and as loved by my family as my sister Heather. I belong. I'm blessed and lucky to be surrounded by the love of my adoptive and stepfamilies, my sons, and my dear close friends. Their love is priceless to me.

I've also realized there's still much to learn on this earth. I will always be a work in progress. There's no finish line, completion, or graduation. I will never reach a point where I have it all figured out. Some of the hardest things we go through, like being adopted or dealing with alcoholism and codependency, can make us more compassionate, understanding, and resilient.

Every time I've let go and let the Universe lead the way, my life has worked out. In contrast, the more I've tried to cling to or force something, the harder it has crashed into failure. One time I heard Dr. Wayne Dyer explain that when you reach into a bucket of water and clench your hands, you can't hold any water. But if you gently cup your hands, you will scoop enough water into your palms to drink. It's the release of force that produces the result. Sometimes we get what we want in life. Sometimes the Universe has a better plan down the road. I'm hopeful for a better plan and have faith that surrendering will lead the way.

In November 2023, I heard Bonnie Garmus speak at an author's lunch about her book *Lessons in Chemistry*, which was made into a series on Hulu. In her book, Garmus tells a powerful story about feminism, strength, and a woman excelling in the male-dominated field of chemistry. Elizabeth Zott, the main character, is working on a degree in chemistry in the 1950s, but a man in power sexually assaults her. After she defends herself during the assault by stabbing him with a pencil, she gets kicked out of the program. Through her daughter's friend, she's offered a cooking show on TV and ends up using the opportunity to teach chemistry through cooking to her in-person audience while also empowering women viewers. This advice from *Lessons in Chemistry* gave me goosebumps of inspiration as I read it:

> Whenever you start doubting yourself, whenever you feel afraid, just remember, courage is the root of change— and make this pledge. No more holding yourself back. No more subscribing to others' opinions of what you can and cannot achieve. And no more allowing anyone to pigeonhole you into useless categories of sex, race, economic status and religion. Do not allow your talents to

lie dormant ladies. Design your own future. When you go home today, ask yourself what will *you* change? And get started.[7]

I feel like I'm just getting started on this new stage of my life. I want to move forward and always be open to change, excited for what the future holds for me. The reading, study, and personal development I've done—including writing my *own* book— have helped me grow exponentially over the past few years. I've worked hard to be happy where I am in life right now. I finally feel grounded in myself. Change takes courage, and I know I've courageously faced fears and struggles that have ultimately led me to myself.

---

[7] Bonnie Garmus, *Lessons in Chemistry* (Penguin Random House, 2022), 360.

Top 5 Books That Have Influenced My Life

Number 1

Tuesdays with Morrie: An Old Man, a Young Man, and Life's Greatest Lesson

by Mitch Albom

Sportswriter and author Mitch Albom tells the true story about getting back in touch with his college professor Morrie Schwartz after seeing Morrie interviewed on *Nightline* about his diagnosis of amyotrophic lateral sclerosis (ALS).

Mitch grows close to Morrie during college but loses touch with him until twenty years later when he sees him on television in March 1995. Learning that Morrie is ill motivates Mitch to reconnect with his mentor and friend. Over the next eight months, Mitch visits Morrie every Tuesday, recording their conversations about death, fear, aging, greed, marriage, family, society, forgiveness, and a meaningful life. Morrie offers Mitch and us, as readers, this wise man's knowledge and experience as he gradually declines from ALS and navigates his own impending death.

This book touched me deeply when I first read it. I'm still awed by how loving Morrie is, even in the depths of a terminal illness. His family and many friends surround him because he's such a loving soul. Morrie and Mitch call the wisdom that Morrie shares his "last lesson" or "thesis."

Reading Morrie's own words about his dying process inspires me (and millions of other readers) to really live and appreciate the joys of life. We all take too much for granted until it's taken away. *Tuesdays with Morrie* is a powerful reminder to live and appreciate the small stuff every day, before it's too late.

Number 2

Codependent No More: How to Stop Controlling Others and Start Caring for Yourself

by Melody Beattie

I first read this book after my dad got sober. I knew my mom had been codependent during their marriage, but it really hit me that I was also codependent in my own marriage to a man who drank too much. I spent years focusing an incredible amount of energy on my husband's behavior and trying to control it instead of caring for myself:

> I am responsible for myself. I am responsible for leading or not living my life. I am responsible for tending to my spiritual, emotional, physical, and financial well-being. I am responsible for identifying and meeting my needs. I am responsible for solving my problems or learning to live with those I cannot solve. I am responsible for my choices. I am responsible for what I give and receive. I am also responsible for setting my goals. I am responsible for how much I enjoy life, for how much pleasure I find in daily activities.[8]

I've read *Codependent No More* numerous times at different points in my life to remind myself that my only job here on earth is to take care of myself. Of course, you have influence over those you care about, and helping them when they're in trouble is part of being in a relationship. But, as the saying goes, you can't help someone who doesn't want to help themself. At the end of the day, we don't get to choose how other people live. We can disagree with their choices and choose to not be around them if that's what's best for us.

This book helped me turn my gaze back on myself and how I wanted to live. I learned that I could choose to listen to myself and my own needs: "Stop looking for happiness in other people. Our source of happiness and well-being is not inside others; it's inside us. Learn to center ourselves in ourselves."[9]

---

[8] Melody Beattie, *Codependent No More: How to Stop Controlling Others and Start Caring for Yourself* (Hazelden, 1986), 114.

[9] Beattie, *Codependent No More*, 107.

Number 3

A Course in Miracles (also called *ACIM* or the *Course*)

edited by Helen Schucman, Bill Thetford, and Kenneth Wapnick

"If you knew Who walks beside you on the way that you have chosen, fear would be impossible."[10]

A Course in Miracles became a significant part of my spiritual growth beginning in 2013. It combines teachings and lessons from Christianity, Judaism, and Buddhism without any dogma. It's a beautiful read that focuses on living from love instead of fear. It has three parts: a text, a workbook with daily readings, and a teaching guide. One main lesson within the book is that we are all teachers as well as students.

I'd heard about *A Course in Miracles* for years. After purchasing a copy, it sat unread on my bookshelf for a long time. Dr. Wayne Dyer and Marianne Williamson—two other self-help, motivational, and spiritual authors and speakers that I respect greatly—both recommended this book, so finally I gave it a read. It's one to digest in small bits and reflect. I joined an *ACIM* study group at my local spiritual center, which further contributed to my growth.

---

[10] Helen Schucman, Bill Thetford, and Kenneth Wapnick, *A Course in Miracles* (Foundation for Inner Peace, 1976), T-18.III.3:2.

Number 4

The Four Agreements: A Practical Guide to Personal Freedom

by Janet Mills and Don Miguel Ruiz

"Nothing other people do is because of you. It is because of themselves. All people live in their own dream, in their own mind; they are in a completely different world from the one we live in."[11]

This self-help book outlines a code of conduct for improving your life based on Toltec teachings, a body of wisdom and spiritual knowledge derived from an ancient civilization in Mesoamerica. A friend recommended it to me years ago, and I've reread it often. The four agreements are:

1. Be impeccable with your word.
2. Don't take anything personally.
3. Don't make assumptions.
4. Always do your best.

The agreements seem simple in theory but applying them in everyday life takes practice and reminders. I have them listed in my bathroom, so I see them every day to remind me. The second agreement, not taking anything personally, has been the most difficult for me to follow. When I was younger, and in my romantic relationships, I took it personally if someone was mean

---

[11] Janet Mills and Don Miguel Ruiz, *The Four Agreements: A Practical Guide to Personal Freedom* (Amber-Allen Publishing, 1997), 48.

to me. Today I still may experience a twinge of hurt, but most of the time I know that everyone is reacting from their own pasts and internal worlds. It's not about me. Even the abuse I experienced was not about me. I've gotten much better at it over time. I let as much as I can roll off my back and actively decide what energy I want to let into my life.

Number 5

The Power of Intention: Learning to Co-Create Your World Your Way

by Dr. Wayne Dyer

More than fifteen years ago, the teachings of Dr. Dyer started me on my journey to change, grow, and create the life I wanted to live. This book lays the foundation for how to deliberately think, in the present, about the future you want to become a reality. Intention is a force in the universe. Everything and everyone are connected to it. Your beliefs are the invisible power behind your intentions. Another key piece of information I learned from him is the importance of changing your perspective about situations beyond your control and letting go of the outcomes, including embracing silence and meditation:

> Practice being in silence and meditation. Nothing relieves stress, depression, anxiety, and all forms of low-energy emotions like silence and meditation. Here, you make conscious contact with your Source and cleanse your connecting link with intention. Take time every day for

moments of quiet contemplation and make meditation a part of your stress-reducing ritual.[12]

I loved listening to Dr. Dyer's books and lectures. I was fortunate to attend a few of his talks at a spiritual retreat called Celebrate Your Life. He also exposed me to meditation and mindfulness, which I still practice to this day. Dr. Dyer wrote many other wonderful books that have changed the lives of millions of people.

---

[12] Wayne Dyer, *The Power of Intention: Learning to Co-Create Your World Your Way* (Hay House, 2004), 214.

Acknowledgments

I want to deeply thank my ghostwriter and publisher, Laura Bush, PhD, of Peacock Proud Press. When we first met, I immediately connected with her. Her expertise and encouragement have meant the world to me. I'm immensely grateful. In the middle of writing this book, Laura's mother passed, and she faced a major health challenge. She continued to make sure this book progressed despite her difficult recovery from surgery. Laura's grace and courage are remarkable. Thank you, also, to Taryn, Chelsey, Kristin, and the entire Peacock Proud Press team.

Thank you to my family for their encouragement and support. I am deeply grateful for each of you and the many beautiful life moments we have shared over the years. I love you all.

Thank you to my dear friends Paula, Andrea, Steffani, Cathy, Shaun and Jim. You have been by my side for many, many years. You're very dear to me, and I love you.

To Club 320, my new friends over the past few years. You're the kindest, warmest group of people. You've shown me that I am not alone in my struggles and how truly strong I am. Thank you for all the wisdom and guidance.

To all the friends in my life who have given me words of encouragement and kept asking me about the progress of the book. I thank you. Your excitement for me writing this book means the world to me.

Thank you to all the counselors and life coaches who have helped me through the years.

Thank you to all the self-help teachers and spiritual authors I have followed over the years. Your teachings and books have influenced me and helped me heal.

Thank you to my sister, Heather, the home-grown baby! You are a bright light in this world, and I'm lucky the Universe brought us together. We are forever connected. I love you.

For my mom, Annie, who raised me. I love you mom. Thank you for loving me. You gave me this poem years ago, and I keep it on my desk:

Not of my flesh, not of my bone
But still miraculously my own
Never forget for a single minute
You didn't grow under my heart, but in it.

For my dad, Glenn, a huge book nerd! Thank you for exposing me to books my entire life. I feel your spirit around me, and I know you are cheering me on. "See" you at the bookstore!

About the Author

L aura Melane is a health and wellness expert with over three decades of experience. Her journey began as a Registered Nurse in hospital and homecare settings before evolving into a multifaceted career focused on fitness and wellness. She founded and grew her own business to help clients of all ages improve their physical and emotional well-being.

With a nursing degree from the University of Washington, Laura holds certifications in personal training from the National Academy of Sports Medicine, Stott Pilates instruction, and sound healing. As a lifelong learner and entrepreneur, she is also a successful real estate investor.

Adopted at birth in Florida, Laura moved to Washington State as a child and later settled in Arizona as an adult. Her personal experiences as a child of adoption have profoundly influenced her work and life. Laura's greatest accomplishment has been healing from lifelong struggles with abandonment, family dysfunction, and codependency, finally finding her authentic identity and voice.

Laura has two wonderful sons and a God-given family she adores. She enjoys practicing yoga, reading in the sun, and spending time with loved ones. Her story is one of resilience, self-discovery, and the power of choosing yourself.

**Laura Melane is available to speak about
her experiences with adoption and codependence.**
Connect with Laura on Instagram @healingsoulwellness